BLESSED AND FAVORED

30 Days, 30 Ways to Surre

Copyright © 2006 by An Sean Fields

Request for information should be addressed to:
Blessed and Favored Publishing,
P.O. Box 15564,
Jersey City, NJ 07305

ISBN-13: 978-0-9791976-0-4
ISBN-10: 0-9791976-0-0

Printed in the United State of America

Cover by: Exodus Design
Photo by: Tamara Cooper/FEMWORKS, LLC

This book is in honor of God, who is the head of my life. I thank Him for choosing me, cleaning me up and planting my feet on the solid ground of His salvation. The Lord is my cornerstone and I shall not be moved.

This book is dedicated to my mother,
Paulette Y. Fields. Although she is not with me in flesh, I know she is with me in spirit. I thank God for His salvation poured upon her, thus granting her eternal life with Him.

In addition, I thank my church, New Beginning Ministries for all their love and support. May God continue to bless and increase them daily, in the name of Jesus.

Words for your Days

Light from you shed arrays of brilliance, wellness, happiness and **holiness**. To who better to confess, love so great you wrap us in **flesh**. You gave us senses to touch, smell, hear, taste, and see your creation. It is truly beautiful, what a sensation. The imprint from your feet shows us our **steps**, if it's your will it is always **right**. To be disobedient is to be grounded, but to obey is to take flight.

You are never **wrong**; you give us peace even when there are storms. Even with our complaining and mocking, your love is constantly **knocking**. The words that you utter to say are what created this very **day**. When we take heed to them, we are **save**d. When we plant them, our **season**s are paved.

What was almost a barely, you turn to a **surely**. Lord, what do we know? To go further we really need your **order**. The adversary pushes hoping we reach our border, but your ways and your words are our menu, once you are with us no matter how we shall **continue**. You are holy and your praise we should always be singing, cause no matter what, joy cometh in the **morning**. The birds don't worry how their going to eat, so we look up for your manna is **sweet**.

Why **doubt** when you have a **set time**, we want it now but you know when it is prime. In you, we can take charge. You in us we are **enlarge**d. We **dress** the outside but it is you, who truly know the inside. You took us across the Red Sea then we **forgot**.

You **fixed** the Jordan for us to cross but we looked back like the wife of Lot. You sent your son, so we can have **living water,** His sheep's shouted master and the wicked shouted slaughter, but for all you laid down your **power**. He is the good shepherd for us, He will go any length. He is the good shepherd He protects us from whoever comes **against**. He gives us a **fresh anointing,** what a wonderful king.

A king who gave will freely, on high but comes low so were never **lonely**. A king who **renew**s and help us on our journeys. His **joy** is **alive** His joy always revives. To him we always need to **pray** meditate and listen to what He says for these are "Words for your days".
- By: Deshawn Cornwall

Table of Contents

Introduction

This book was birthed out of my online blog, "Word of the Day", which is daily inspirational messages meant to be encouraging, thought provoking and assist in helping the new or mature Christian gain a deeper understanding of Christ Jesus, the covenant of God and our contribution to our own spiritual growth. It is through the daily mediation on Gods word that allows each Christian to grow and mature into the person God wants us to become. For the word of God is living and active. Sharper than any double-edged sword, it penetrates even to dividing soul and spirit, joints and marrow; it judges the thoughts and attitudes of the heart (Hebrews 4:12). Therefore, we as Christians must have a made up mind that we want to do right in the Lord.

In order to conclude that we want heaven to be our final destination, we sometimes have to go through situations, trials and tribulations. When we do go through these circumstances, it's the word of God that allows us to stand, go through and come out. This word must be consumed daily, understood and put into action. We must be doers of the word and not just listeners.

Let us pray: Dear Lord, as I begin to read this written word, I ask you to open my ears, my eyes, my mind, my spirit, my soul and my heart to receive the special message you have for my life. I come, Lord, in search of a deeper connection to your love and grace. Hoping to be transformed into the person, you would have me to become. Speak to me, Father, in the name of Jesus. Amen.

In the beginning was the **Word**, and the **Word** was with God, and the **Word** was God.

-John 1:1

Word of the Day – Light!

Genesis 1:4
"God saw that the **light** was good, and He separated the light from the darkness."

Exodus 13:21
"By day the LORD went ahead of them in a pillar of cloud to guide them on their way and by night in a pillar of fire to give them **light**, so that they could travel by day or night."

2 Samuel 22:29
"You are my lamp, O LORD; the LORD turns my darkness into **light**."

Matthew 5:16
"In the same way, let your **light** shine before men, that they may see your good deeds and praise your Father in heaven."

Jesus is the way, the truth and the life. No man comes to the father, except through Jesus, says John 14:6. Having Jesus in your heart is like someone lighting a match in a darkness-filled cellar. It brightens the way and allows for your escape. That is exactly what surrendering to Christ is like to those coming out of the world. It's like someone made a way for your escape and that someone is Jesus Christ. What are you escaping, one might ask. You're escaping the pains of this world, anxiety, depression, poverty, unemployment, bondage, and other elements which hold us captive but most importantly the death penalty. For the wages of sin is death (Romans 6:23) but through Christ you have eternal life.

It's crucial to understand that Christ died on the cross so that our sins would be wiped away and thrown into the sea of forgetfulness. He died to free us from bondage, thus reconciling us back to God, for our sins separated us from His glory. When Jesus died, and rose on the third day, we were restored to purity, as it was in the beginning with Adam and Eve. We were restored and given eternal life; as long as we believed in the precious name of Jesus Christ and turned away from our previous sins, never to revisit them again but instead start a new Christ filled life. Our lives must be filled with Christ inside and out, if we expect to stand firm in our faith and against the wiles of the devil. For, just as the light of a candle may begin to fade or blinker and finally go out completely when the supporting elements have diminished, so will our faith. This is why we must stay connected to the power source, which is God, so that our light never goes out but shines brighter and brighter as we spend more time in prayer and fasting.

Through these things, your light will no doughtily begin to shine for all those around you to look on with amazement. For the person that once was, will be no more. You'll now have a heavenly glow of serenity, which no one can take away because it comes from above. It comes from a man-child that gave His life, died on a cross for our sins and rose to take His rightful place on the right hand of God. This man-child is Jesus, the king of all kings.

Christ is the true light and the vine that connects us directly to God. Some don't believe in Him but I've experienced His miraculous power first hand. Therefore, I say to those unbelievers, don't knock'em until you try Him. He truly has been a light in my dark days and a breath of fresh air in my new days. See,

I've tried others but found none as trustworthy as He. I prayed to others but found none as loyal as He. I've sought others but found none more rewarding as He. This is why I worship Him, so. He's been so much and done so much for me and I just know that as you begin your journey with Christ He will do the same for you.

Dear Lord, as I seek your face give me the strength to endure all things. Expose your mercy and grace. Order my steps on the path you would have me to go. I humble myself to you to take control. In the name of Jesus, I pray. Amen.

Word of the Day – Holiness!

Exodus 15:11
"Who among the gods is like you, O LORD ? Who is like you— majestic in **holiness**, awesome in glory, working wonders?"

Psalm 29:2
"Ascribe to the LORD the glory due his name; worship the LORD in the splendor of his **holiness**."

Psalm 93:5
"Your statutes stand firm; **holiness** adorns your house for endless days, O LORD."

Isaiah 35:8
"And a highway will be there; it will be called the Way of **Holiness**. The unclean will not journey on it; it will be for those who walk in that Way; wicked fools will not go about on it."

The road to Christ is a holy walk. No man can partake of the walk, unless he affirms his mind and spirit to the ways of Jesus. You have to come to a point where you no longer want to do the things that separates you from the love of God. Yes, it's a holy walk and Jesus is the perfect example of how to take that walk, while living and serving God. He walked upright, preaching and teaching the gospel to those in need. He healed the masses, which wanted deliverance. He feed those that needed to be fed, not only in the natural with bread but also in the spiritual with the Word of God. However, as scripture depicts, the people wanted healing, deliverance and to be set free. They came out in the masses looking for something and found the mercy of God. God has repeatedly told me that those people wanted

- 4 -

something special. Jesus didn't have to beg, plead or argue with anyone to get them to come out for their deliverance. The Word spread across the villages, come see a man that can set you free of sickness and disease and the people came out in crowds.

As Jesus walked the streets of Galilee, some ran to Him for a healing, a miracle or deliverance. While others just watched, the blessings pour upon those in search. They sat there holding on to their excuses and doubt. Some didn't want to be set free and most importantly, they didn't want any part of Christ. Some even thought what they were doing was right, like the Pharisee. This is exactly how people are today. In just writing this message, I feel bad for those who are ignorant to the Word of God. It hurts because they truly don't know their fate. They don't know that Hebrews 12:14 says, "without holiness no one will see the Lord." That means, not me, not you, not your mother, not your sister, not your father, not your brother, not anyone unless they conform to the spirit of God. That's why it's imperative to have the Holy Spirit, because He teaches you how to live holy. He teaches you how to walk in the will of God. He's a keeper, a sanctifier, comforter and a counselor. Without the Holy Spirit, you're walking in self and flesh which leads to damnation.

"Whosoever therefore resisteth the power (Holy Spirit), resisteth the ordinance of God: and they that resist shall receive to themselves damnation." - Romans 13:2

See, I'm not making this stuff up. It's all in the Word of God. Holiness is a requirement for everyone, not just those that teach and preach the gospel. It's for everyone that wants to see Jesus and kneel at the feet of God, praising His holy name. It took me a few years to walk right before God but now that I am, I love Him even the more. Because I don't feel ashamed to be in His presence but in fact find it a privilege. I know some wonder, how I know I am walking upright. I know because I don't read the bible, I put the Word into action. I have transformed my life to the words of God. Am I perfect? No, but I'm letting God perfect me more and more everyday. The more I praise Him the more He perfects me. The more I call on Him, the more He perfects my walk. The more I acknowledge my sins and repent, the more He cleans me up. Don't you want to be clean? Don't you want to walk in holiness? I do.

Lord, teach me to walk in holiness. Teach me, dear Lord to walk as Christ once did. Give me a repenting heart, which will call on you in times of trouble. Cleanse me, dear Lord, from the crown of my head to the sole of my feet. Hear my prayer and begin working in my life. In the name of Jesus, amen.

Word of the Day – Flesh!

Psalm 73:26
"My **flesh** and my heart may fail, but God is the strength of my heart and my portion forever."

John 6:51
"I am the living bread that came down from heaven. If anyone eats of this bread, he will live forever. This bread is my **flesh**, which I will give for the life of the world."

John 6:63
"The Spirit gives life; the **flesh** counts for nothing. The words I have spoken to you are spirit and they are life."

Ephesians 6:12
"For our struggle is not against **flesh** and blood, but against the rulers, against the authorities, against the powers of this dark world and against the spiritual forces of evil in the heavenly realms."

This softness around these bones is the corruptible flesh that calls us to sin and violate the laws that govern the rights of passage into heaven. You see the flesh doesn't care where the soul or any other part of the body goes when the expiration date is up because the flesh is only interested in instant gratification. The flesh is looking for right now results. It's looking for now sex, now finances, now organisms, now house, now husband, now wife, now employment, now children, now fulfillment, instead of now patience and now faith.

It's patience that produces the faith to believe God is working things out to your good. If your patient right now, then by faith you know you have the victory. To build patience, you have to put your flesh under the subjection of your mind. In order to do this your mind has to be stayed on Jesus. Jesus has to be your complete focus in order to overthrow the flesh, thus conquering that which is directly connected to you and is a main threat to your survival in Christ. You see, the flesh and the spirit are constantly at war with each other. Each wanting to control the other but we know the winner must be the spirit, if we are to receive eternal life. This is why the Apostle Paul said, "But I discipline my body and bring it into subjection, lest, when I have preached to others, I myself should become disqualified. (1 Corinthians 9:27, NKJV)"

We must discipline our body through prayer and fasting. Prayer is communion with God. It's a sacred conversation in which we express our need for spiritual cleansing, the need to be made whole and the need for His grace, which will help us through the battle of the flesh. Fasting disciplines the body to rely on the Word of God instead of natural instinct. Therefore, I urge each of you to starve the body of that which has become a major part of your life. Separate yourself from television, food, phone calls, sleep or possibly constant time with others and get alone. For it's in the alone state that God can really work in you and manifest Himself. It's in the spirit that God can reveal His glory. We all must crucify our flesh daily or it will crucify us; sending our souls to a place where even the devil is fighting not to go.

Lord, crucify this flesh and let your Holy Spirit rise inside of me. Manifest your spirit in my flesh, so that it will never rise up against me. Create in me a clean heart with a do right mind stayed on Christ as I seek your holy name. In the name of Jesus, I pray. Amen.

Word of the Day – Step!

Deuteronomy 21:5
*"The priests, the sons of Levi, shall **step** forward, for the LORD your God has chosen them to minister and to pronounce blessings in the name of the LORD and to decide all cases of dispute and assault."*

Job 23:11
*"My feet have closely followed his **steps**; I have kept to his way without turning aside."*

Psalm 17:5
*My **steps** have held to your paths; my feet have not slipped.*

Jeremiah 10:23
*"I know, O LORD, that a man's life is not his own; it is not for man to direct his **steps**."*

I have stepped forward to receive all my blessings from God, knowing that He loves me so much and He desires to shower me with His very best. See, I have learned that mere man cannot take care of me. I have learned that mere woman cannot nurture me. Only the one true Living God can provide all things. Only He can lift my head out of bed. Only He can give me the desires of my heart. Yes, I have had men and women give me many things. I've gotten flowers, cars, furs, furniture, peripherals, and money but none of those things come close to what God has given me; eternal life. Through Christ, my sins are forgiven and I have a second chance to be with the Father. I have a second chance to get my walk with Christ right. I have a second chance to live holy in this present world. You don't know how that feels, unless you too were once on death row. You don't know how it feels to be restored, unless you too were once smothered in sin.

It's therefore the reason that I hold fast to the promises of God, allowing Him to order my steps and lead me wherever He pleases. For I know that wherever He takes me, the land will be filled with milk and honey. I know that wherever He leads me, the streets will be paved with gold and my storehouse will overflow with blessings.

I can stand on these promises because of my life before God. I can stand on these promises because of my obedience. I can stand on these promises because I don't come with excuses, explanations, hang-ups, unjust causes or anything else that will separate me from God. For I'm clinging to God for dear life, knowing that He is my everything. I'm stepping out on faith, knowing that He won't let me fall. After all, He said, "He shall never leave me nor forsake me (Joshua 1:5b)". I hold tight to these words because they are true, just like God.

Dear Lord, I step into your hands and let you have your way in my life. Do to me, as you will. I trust the plans you have for my life. I trust the destination you have for my path. Lead me, as you would have me to go, heavenly Father. In Jesus name, I pray that you have your way. Amen.

Word of the Day – Right!

Genesis 4:7
"If you do what is **right**, will you not be accepted? But if you do not do what is **right**, sin is crouching at your door; it desires to have you, but you must master it."

Exodus 15:6
"Your **right** hand, O LORD, was majestic in power. Your **right** hand, O LORD, shattered the enemy."

Joshua 23:6
"Be very strong; be careful to obey all that is written in the Book of the Law of Moses, without turning aside to the **right** or to the left."

Psalm 19:8
"The precepts of the LORD are **right**, giving joy to the heart. The commands of the LORD are radiant, giving light to the eyes."

The precepts of the Lord are right. In the same manner, holiness and righteousness is right, adding to the precepts of the Lord. I once thought going to church and worshipping God would be enough to receive His protection, blessings and love. However, it takes more than that. People can follow the Ten Commandments and still land themselves in hell. Why? Well, because it takes more than not stealing, honoring your mother and father and not giving false testimony to make it into heaven. It takes commitment, love, faithfulness, understanding, dedication, and obedience. In this walk with Christ, you must stand firm on all the principles, you're being taught. You must not sway between right and wrong but choose a side.

"No man can serve two masters: for either he will hate the one, and love the other; or else he will hold to the one, and despise the other. Ye cannot serve God and mammon. "- Matthew 6:24 (KJV)

This is why it's important to understand the requirements for rightful living, which include not only the Ten Commandments but holiness and righteousness. Holiness is separating yourself from the images of the world; reserved for Christ. It doesn't mean to discontinue communication or socializing with those that are not seeking God in the same way as you but to be an example of the glory of God. This means ending sexual relationships and either consider marriage or mere friendship, thus eliminating all intimacy. This also means no sweet talk; no late night calls, no spending the night, and no snuggling up with each other. Either your partner wants all of you including your love of Christ and determination to be a light to the world or they want to continue down their old path of destruction. If they are not embracing the new person God has created in you and not respecting your newfound values, then you must let them proceed on their path alone, praying that God will touch their heart. For as Christians, we want all of our family, friends and loved ones to find Christ and have the eternal life promised. However, until they conclude that they want Christ, we must continue on our quest for Jesus alone.

Ending a relationship, in which feelings are involved, is really a tough step to endure but it's a sacrifice that God honors and never forgets. When I came to Christ and surrendered 100%, I was in a wonderful relationship. I thought this man was great and wanted to be his wife, spending the rest of my life with him. With this man, my daughter and I both felt like we were a family. That's why it was so hard for me to give him up when God revealed what I was doing was wrong and outside of His will because He wanted me all the way. He wanted me to purify myself and become clean again, through the sacrifice, and purging of my sin. I thought letting go of the man I was dating was going to kill me, so I kept holding on. Even after, I ended the sexual part our relationship he continued to come over for weekends and I would take him to church as an attempt to justify my stubbornness. I thought the more he saw me yielding to God, the more he would want to do the same but instead it drove a wedge between us. The closer I got to God, the more we became distant. We no longer spoke the same language. We no longer wanted the same things out of life. I wanted all of God and he was a frightened little boy that was still holding on to his past, instead of letting God heal him. He was holding on to the memories of his absentee father, his past substance abuse, past relationships and past wasted time that he could never recapture. I was reaching for the new, for the future and for all the splendor of God. The more I glowed with praise, the more uncomfortable he became with me. The more I was filled with the Holy Spirit, the more he withdrew and it got to a point where he no longer wanted to be around me. Therefore, he ended the friendship stating, he didn't want God the same as me. I thanked him for setting my heart free and I've been focused on Jesus all the way. My heart didn't break after all and I found a whole new relationship with God. Although, the split didn't feel right in my flesh, it felt right in my soul and God opened up to me even more, revealing that He was the true owner of my heart.

I share this with you in hopes that you will see the need to walk on the path God has chosen for you and allow Him to take control of your heart, your life and environment. After all, He's the one that gave you life, for not only is He the owner but He's the creator.

Dear God, may you come into my life and bless me like never before. Heal me from past hurts and protect my heart. For it's you that I put all my hope and trust in. You're my strength when I am weak. You're my breath, when I can't breathe. I love you with all my heart, in the name of Jesus, I pray. Amen.

List the things and people that you need to let go!

Things I need to let go for God:

_____

_____

_____

_____

_____

_____

_____

_____

_____

People I need to let go for God.

_____

_____

_____

_____

_____

_____

_____

_____

_____

Lord, may you lead me into your presence. May you guide me into your prefect will. Keep your hand of favor upon my life and protect me from evil. Increase my borders on every side that I may serve you freely and do the good work you have ordained over my life. I surrender all, I give you my best, and I put all my trust in your holy name. I praise you and glorify you. I pray in Jesus holy name, amen.

Word of the Day – Wrong!

Numbers 5:6
"Say to the Israelites: 'When a man or woman **wrongs** another in any way and so is unfaithful to the LORD, that person is guilty"

Deuteronomy 32:4
"He is the Rock, his works are perfect, and all his ways are just. A faithful God who does no **wrong**, upright and just is he."

Nehemiah 9:33
"In all that has happened to us, you have been just; you have acted faithfully, while we did **wrong**."

Psalm 119:104
"I gain understanding from your precepts; therefore I hate every **wrong** path."

We can't correct the wrongs of our past. We can't make up for lost time, correct dead situations or redo past decisions. However, we can make a new commitment to press forward and look to the new light that Christ has imparted within us. For we all have done some wrong in our former lives before we met Christ. I myself was involved in several sexual relationships. It meant nothing for me to go to a male's house, have sex, and spend the night or even the weekend. It was a part of who I was at that time. In fact, I had sex so much until one day I couldn't even have an orgasm. I was all out of them. I should have known at that point enough was enough but I continued to dwell in my mess, called life. Can I correct that wrong? No. I can't undo all the men that I was intimately involved with. However, I can make sure that other women and men know to save themselves until marriage. I can give my testimony on how sex was killing me spiritually and physically. I can share with women about the satisfaction and reward in waiting on God to deliver on His promises, whether it is a husband, a house, a car, a renewed spirit, a reversed health condition, or anything you want. God is the ultimate corrector of all wrong, once you give your life to Him.

While I was out in the world, I suffered many things. Heartbreak, poverty, unemployment, disease, bankruptcy, mental abuse, physical abuse and many other effects of the world. Some I thought would destroy me and others I thought would haunt me for the rest of my life but the blood of Jesus covered me. There's power in the blood that was shed on Calvary. There is power in the name of Mary's baby because when I called on Jesus, He erased every wrong, He wiped my slate clean, He dusted me off and set my feet on solid ground. That's why I can't look back now, not even if I wanted to look back. I can't turn around, not even if I wanted to go in reverse because God has altered that which is no more. The alterations are made inside me. The new interior is the Word stored up in my soul. The new exterior is the glory of God on my face. It's in my new walk, my new talk and it's all in my new attitude, that Jesus is Lord. Hallelujah!

Therefore, I don't dwell on my past and the wrong roads I have traveled on. I chalk it all up to a young woman that was lost in the wilderness looking for a way out. Then one day on that yellow brick road, I met up with the Father, the Son and the Holy Ghost. They became my confidants, my comforters, my suppliers, my redeemers, my restorers and everything I would ever need. Now that I have them, I can do no wrong because I don't think on the wrong things of this world. I keep my eyes fixed on Jesus, so that I don't get disqualified in the end. I keep my eyes in the bible because I don't want to know what the next man is doing; thus stirring up unwelcome feelings. I keep my eyes straight ahead, focused on the prize, which is Christ.

Dear Lord, I thank you for all the promises you have for my life and I know that you will fulfill all of them in your due time. I need only wait on you and while waiting walk in all holiness and righteousness. I thank you for your mercy that endures forever and ever. In Jesus name, Amen.

Word of the Day – Knocking!

Song of Solomon 5:2
"[Beloved] I slept but my heart was awake. Listen! My lover is **knocking**: "Open to me, my sister, my darling, my dove, my flawless one. My head is drenched with dew, my hair with the dampness of the night."

Matthew 7:7(NKJV)
"[Keep Asking, Seeking, **Knocking**] "Ask, and it will be given to you; seek, and you will find; knock, and it will be opened to you."

Luke 11:10 (AMP)
"For everyone who asks and keeps on asking receives; and he who seeks and keeps on seeking finds; and to him who knocks and keeps on **knocking**, the door shall be opened."

Luke 13:25
"Once the owner of the house gets up and closes the door, you will stand outside **knocking** and pleading, 'Sir, open the door for us.' "But he will answer, 'I don't know you or where you come from.'"

God was knocking on my door for years, trying to get into my life and enrich me with all the qualities of a virtuous woman. Somehow, I would either ignore the knocks at the door or shake it off as my mind playing tricks on me. After all, who would believe someone like me would turn over a new leaf? Now that I have finally succumbed to my calling for a deeper relationship with Christ, I feel spiritually awakened. I feel alive. I feel like the sky is the limit and I can jump over a rainbow. I finally opened the door for God to step in and now I can breathe again, I can sing, I can dance and I can be who I want to be in the name of Jesus Christ. It's an indescribable feeling. For with Christ for us, who can be against us? No one!

Yes, the tables have turned and now I'm the one doing the knocking. I am knocking on the gates of heaven, saying, "let me in". I am knocking on the door to prosperity, saying, "Here I is". I am knocking on the supply keeper's door, saying, "Fill me up with all I need". Then, I'm going down to the shareholders office and say, "I've been a good girl, please send His mercy, glory, grace and goodness to me". I'm going to let holiness and righteousness preceded me, so people know I'm coming. I'm going to put on my tiara, which is the glow of complete salvation to accentuate the crown of my face.

Will my Lord turn me away? Will He not answer the door for His princess? I finally said, yes to His will and His ways. I'm finally living without a man, turning over at night to my bible and prayers raveling off in my mind. I study His word and follow His every lead. Have I been disobedient in my walk? If so, please point it out, so that I can remove any sin that separates me from you. Have I steered off the road to righteousness? If so, please correct me so I can get back on the right track and seek you even the more. Tell me if I've asked for too much. Tell me if I don't deserve to have my heart desires fulfilled. Tell me where I've gone wrong and where I need to go right. I'm at the point of no return. I don't know any other way but to serve the Lord. It seems as if the world has changed drastically since I was last out there. People don't seem the same anymore; they seem to be even worse. The music isn't the same, since I last listened; it seems to have more sexual content than before. The men aren't the same; they seem to be weaker than I remember. You see, I can't go back. Therefore, I have no other choice but to press on, in hope that when I do knock at your door Father, you'll answer with a smile. Please don't rebuke me, nor forsake the sight of me. I'm yours all the way; do, as you want to me. I'm yours all the way, bless or not bless me as you want. I'm yours all the way, heal or not heal me. I'm yours all the way. Yours for the taking. Yours for the caring. Yours for the keeping. Yours for the loving. Yours all the way.

Dear Lord, I am knocking at your door, seeking shelter in your wings of protection. Stretch out to me and comfort me. You are the rock of my foundation and without you I have nothing. Continue to be with me, as I depend on you in all my ways. In the name of Jesus, Amen.

Word of the Day – Day!

Ezra 9:15
"O LORD, God of Israel, you are righteous! We are left this **day** as a remnant. Here we are before you in our guilt, though because of it not one of us can stand in your presence."

Psalm 25:5
"guide me in your truth and teach me, for you are God my Savior, and my hope is in you all **day** long."

Psalm 27:4
"One thing I ask of the LORD, this is what I seek: that I may dwell in the house of the LORD all the **days** of my life, to gaze upon the beauty of the LORD and to seek him in his temple."

Psalm 35:28
"My tongue will speak of your righteousness and of your praises all **day** long."

As I continue on my path to be a Christ like woman of God, I know there are some things I am going to encounter. There's going to be people that will argue a woman's role in ministry, try to hold me back or not support my projects, goals and ideas. When I think of the obstacles I will have to overcome, it's somewhat disheartening and at the same time overwhelming but I thank God my trust is not in any of the naysayer's but in Him. My trust is in the truth I know about the character of God. I know for a fact, He's a rescuer. I know for a fact, He doesn't abandon those who love Him. I know for a fact, He doesn't leave you out in the desert without a way out. No, God doesn't do any of those things, which are the things most people do to one another. So, what do I have to be afraid or

intimidated about? I only need to praise God and call
on Him each and every day.

We have to soak our lives in prayer. Prayer has to
become a daily part of your routine. As Christians, we
are soldiers for the Lord because there is a spiritual
war going on around us. The war is between God
and Satan. The devil is trying to pull every Saint out
from under the covenant of God because he wants as
many recruits in his army as possible. He believes
this is the winning tactic to overthrow God. He
continues to underestimate the power of the Lord. He
still thinks that he can out power, out wit and out rank
the Lord; strong and mighty. When Satan was kicked
out of heaven, he continued to be just as arrogant and
believe that he can exalt himself over God. That's
why we must pray and praise God at all times,
*"because your adversary the devil, as a roaring lion,
walketh about, seeking whom he may devour"* (1
Peter 5:8 KJV).

The saints of God have to be strong. We must also,
be on guard and continue to uplift everyone in prayer.
Prayer is the shield that keeps the enemy at bay.
Prayer is a supernatural force that produces results,
not only in heavenly realms but also made manifest in
the natural. Prayer changes not only the atmosphere
around you but it changes medical results, it changes
your financial situations, it changes your husband,
kids, problems, and attitude. For I know that when I
get down on my knees in prayer God is going to
respond. It may not be today, it may not be tomorrow
but I know that in due season, God is going to pour
out what's rightfully mine. I know that God is a prayer
answering God, especially if you're walking upright
before Him and serving Him the best way you know
how. This is how I'm living today. I'm serving Him the

best way I possibly know how and living the best way I know how to live before Him. I've sacrificed; I've given up some things, and some people. God can't fail me now. God can't turn a deaf ear to me. He has to hear my prayer and because I know He heard my plea, then I know He has to answer it. Now here comes the true act of faith; waiting on God to deliver on your prayers. This is truly, where the faith comes into play- waiting. Sometimes weeks, months, then sometimes just a day but either way I have to wait. If you can't tell, this is one of my weak points – longsuffering.

Yes, God requires a waiting period for some things to manifest in our lives. Not because He cannot resolve the problem right away but just to see if we are willing to wait. Just to test how badly we want it. Just to see if we love Him as we say we do. Just to find out if we really feel it's worth the wait. To ensure we're ready for the blessing. Can we handle it. That's why I'm careful about the requests I put before the Lord. I make sure I provide as much detail as possible and I'm very specific about what I want. I don't want to say, Lord please provide me a car and end up with a 1950 Lincoln that only goes 10 mph. Now, not that there's anything wrong with having an older car but if I have to drive my daughter around, get to work and run errands, I need a car that moves faster than 10 mph. That's why I'm very specific in my prayers. I don't just say, Lord, I need a financial blessing. I say, Lord, I need one million dollars and 55 cents. This is how you get the amount you want instead of 35 cents, which is still a blessing. Praise God. Anything and everything that comes from heaven is a blessing, know matter how small and minuet it may seem, it's a blessing because He didn't have to do it but He did.

Therefore, as you go throughout the day, lift your hands in prayer to the Lord. Whether out loud or silently to yourself, pray to God and rejoice in His Love. Think about all He has done from you, where He's brought you from and then glean to where He's taking you. Sure, some of it seem a little uncertain but remember God has a plan for each and every one of us. Our futures are bright as long as we continue to put God first and stay connected to His Love.

Dear Lord, I thank you for waking me up today, for someone found themselves being received into your bosom. I thank you Lord, for the good works that you have started in me and pray that you finish them. Please continue to work in me, as I continue to dwell in your presence. With all the love of Christ, I pray to you in Jesus name. Amen.

Word of the Day – Save!

Psalm 138:7
"Though I walk in the midst of trouble, you preserve my life; you stretch out your hand against the anger of my foes, with your right hand you **save** me."

Psalm 146:3
"Do not put your trust in princes, in mortal men, who cannot **save**."

Isaiah 33:22
"For the LORD is our judge, the LORD is our lawgiver, the LORD is our king; it is he who will **save** us."

Luke 19:10
"For the Son of Man came to seek and to **save** what was lost."

We are the lost sheep that Jesus came to save from the snare of the enemy. We are the chosen people that Jesus wants to reconcile back to the Father, thus redeeming our souls from the clutches of the devil and freeing us to worship God without a spot or a blemish of sin. For Jesus was the innocent lamb, led to the slaughter for the sins of the world. We owe everything we have to Jesus Christ. He is the savior of our souls. For we were supposed to have endured the pain, beatings and punishment that He underwent but we didn't. We were supposed to be that blood stained body pinned to a cross but we weren't. Jesus paid the ultimate price for all of our sins. He died so that we could be set free. Yes, He saved us from the death penalty.

He only asks that we put our sins aside and come unto Him. He has freed us from the adversary. Why would we want to go back? Why would anyone want to go back on death row? Yet, that's what we do when we choose to go back to sin or continue to sin in the midst of our Christian walk. That's why I'm asking everyone to stop, look and listen. Stop what you're doing that goes against the will of God. Stop sinning and look at the sacrifice of Christ on the cross. Look around you at those that are dying from the sins of their life. Look at how drugs, HIV, alcohol, pregnancy, STD's and other elements are at an all times high in most communities around the country. Listen to what God is telling all of us about turning our lives over to Him. Listen to His promise for a better life, healings, prosperity, joy, happiness, abundance and other miraculous blessings.

These things are within our reach, if we want God to save us from ourselves, because for most of us, we are our own worst enemy. I believe we are our own enemy because we succumb to our own internal thoughts. We succumb to the whispers of the enemy, to the world around us and to the pressures of friends and family. Furthermore, we lack the knowledge and wisdom to use the power of Christ to save ourselves.

God is not telling us not to have fun. On the contrary, Jesus stated, "I am come that they might have life, and that they might have it more abundantly (John 10:10b KJV). Therefore, He wants us to enjoy our lives here on earth. However, He wants us to have love and peace in our hearts. He wants us to care for our fellow men, women and children. For if, we truly loved each other, would you let another starve? If we truly loved each other, could we steal from another man? If we truly love each other, could you see another go homeless? No, love wouldn't let any of those things occur. I love my mother and only want the best for her. If she didn't have food, I would take her some groceries. If she didn't have shelter, she would move in with me and I would never steal a dime from her. Love would not allow such mistreatment. Love is worth more than that, it's more precious than that and it doesn't work like that.

Dear Lord, teach us first how to save ourselves and then how to save the ones we love. Teach us how to be humble and summit ourselves as a living sacrifice unto you. Teach us how to rescue those around us and help them to receive salvation through Christ Jesus. In Jesus holy name, I pray. Amen.

Word of the Day – Season!

Deuteronomy 28:12
"The LORD will open the heavens, the storehouse of his bounty, to send rain on your land in **season** and to bless all the work of your hands. You will lend to many nations but will borrow from none."

Ecclesiastes 3:1
"[A Time for Everything] There is a time for everything, and a **season** for every activity under heaven:"

Jeremiah 8:7
"Even the stork in the sky knows her appointed **season**s, and the dove, the swift and the thrush observe the time of their migration. But my people do not know the requirements of the LORD. "

Titus 1:3
"and at his appointed **season** he brought his word to light through the preaching entrusted to me by the command of God our Savior,"

This is a new season. Some say this is the season where God fixes everything in our lives. It's the season of correcting your attitude, correcting your finances, correcting the church and setting it in order, correcting our behavior, correcting our target of love, correcting our direction, and our ways. Some say that this is the season of prosperity. It's the season where all your finances are released. It's the season where you get the house you've been praying for, it's the season in which you pay off all your bills, it's the season for your new car, it's the season of no more living from pay check to pay check, it's the season of good health, it's the season of miraculous healings, it's the season of claiming what you want and receiving it. Well, I say it's simply your season!

It's your season to do, receive and get whatever you want from God, from this world, for yourself, your family and your friends. However, there's a catch to this being your season. Yes, there's a catch to everything. However, I wouldn't call this a catch but more a requirement that was established since the beginning of time. The requirement is you to live as if you want God to bless you. You have to act as if you want God to bless you. You have to talk as if you want God to bless you. You have to walk as if you want God to bless you. For some this may require a complete overhaul, while for others this simply means you need to re-establish some of your principles or recommit yourself to God. Yes, it's the "You" season. It's time for you to do you, seek things for yourself, be yourself, treat yourself and love yourself. It's time for you to seek God to make you over. Seek God to change all the things about yourself that's unpleasing to you. It's your season, it's your time. I can't stop saying that. Yes, it's all about you sweetie.

It also means that it's my season too. It's my time to shine. It's my time to be blessed. It's my time for peace of mind. It's my time for laughter. It's my time to travel. It's my time to step out and trust God all the way in my hopes and dreams. I don't know about you but I want to do something outrageous. I want to do the unthinkable. I want to let God take me all the way up. I want to give God a radical praise. I want to give Him an outrageous offering. I want to do a drastic fast. I want to pray a 3 hour prayer, going in and out of the spirit. I want to let God know that I love Him with all my heart and thank Him for making this my season. I've been faithful all year round. I've been seeking Him everyday. I've been serving in His house. I've been sacrificing when necessary and when asked. I've been listening for His voice and obeying His word. I've been as obedient as I know how. I've stood when I wanted to fall and it's finally my season.

Therefore, I urge each of you to claim your season. Praise God for the things He's about to unleash in your life. Worship Him for who He is. Who is He? He's:

El SHADDAI - God All
JEHOVAH-JIREH - The Lord will provide
JEHOVAH-ROHI - The Lord Our Shepherd
I AM - I AM the Light of the world

He's the God that never changes nor ceases to respond to our prayers.

Lord, show me how to worship you in season and out of season. Help me subject my feelings to my mind. Active my faith in you, dear Lord. Please remove all stumbling blocks from my path, so that I can praise you as a bold soldier. In the name of Jesus. Amen

.

Word of the Day – Surely!

Genesis 32:12
"But you have said, 'I will **surely** make you prosper and will make your descendants like the sand of the sea, which cannot be counted.' "

Genesis 50:25
"And Joseph made the sons of Israel swear an oath and said, "God will **surely** come to your aid, and then you must carry my bones up from this place."

Job 14:16
"**Surely** then you will count my steps but not keep track of my sin."

Psalm 32:6
"Therefore let everyone who is godly pray to you while you may be found; **surely** when the mighty waters rise, they will not reach him."

I surely don't deserve all the good things God has done for me. Not only did He send His only begotten Son to save a wretch like me but He also freed me from bondage, shook all the sin off me, and turned me around onto solid ground. Surely, the Lord, mighty and strong loves all of us, despite our shortcomings. He must look at us as little images of perfection that have gone astray for one reason or another and onto different paths. However, although we may stray, the spirit of the Lord watches over us. Yes, the Lord watches over all of His sheep whether we acknowledge Him or not. That's what I love about the Lord. Even if you don't live right and even if you never call on His name, He still watches over you. See the Lord knows that whether you acknowledge Him now or later, you will surrender. For the word says, that every knee shall bow and every tongue confess that He is Lord. Therefore, you can confess it now or later. It's up to you when you do it but it's surely going to be confessed when Christ returns.

Yes, there's going to be a second coming of Christ. My spirit is telling me Jesus Christ is going to return and it's not that long off. He's ready to come and show the glory of God but He moves when God tells Him to move and God hasn't issued the command just yet. God is waiting for some of us to get it right, voluntarily surrender, to turn from our evil ways, to receive the fullness of the Holy Spirit that will allow us to be caught up in the rapture.

Surely, goodness and mercy shall follow me all the days of my life because I finally understand that my life here on earth is not about me or about my family but about Jesus. It's about doing the work of Him that sent me. It's about allowing God to work through me to set the captives free. To bring those that have been scattered back into the hands of the owner, who is Jehovah. For I am just the mere hired hand that doesn't own the sheep but through my love, I care and gather the sheep on behalf of it's owner. Who is the owner of all the sheep? The Good Shepherd, Elohim. For surely, He would lay down His life to save one sheep that has gone astray. Can you say the same?

Dear Lord, surely goodness and mercy shall follow me all the days of my life. Surely, Lord, you hear me and wish to answer every pray that I lift up to you. Forgive me of all sin, whether seen or unseen in my eyesight and plant my feet on solid ground as I seek you through your word. In the name of Jesus, amen.

Word of the Day – Order!

Numbers 9:23
"At the LORD's command they encamped, and at the LORD's command they set out. They obeyed the LORD's **order**, in accordance with his command through Moses."

Matthew 12:44
"Then it says, 'I will return to the house I left.' When it arrives, it finds the house unoccupied, swept clean and put in **order**."

Luke 4:36
"All the people were amazed and said to each other, "What is this teaching? With authority and power he gives **order**s to evil spirits and they come out!"

Romans 7:4
"So, my brothers, you also died to the law through the body of Christ, that you might belong to another, to him who was raised from the dead, in **order** that we might bear fruit to God."

As I put my life into perspective and give everything its proper order, I wonder if I'm doing too much or not enough to please God. I don't believe there's such a thing as doing to much for God but one can do too much in one area thus leaving other areas lacking. This is why I'm taking inventory of myself, yet again. I want to ensure that I'm balancing it all out. I want to be well rounded in my Christian walk. I don't want to be the jack of all trades and the master of none but I want a full understanding of the different offices and then specialize in one or a few, based on where God calls me.

I strongly believe that all of us, whether we recognize it or not have a ministry within us. We all have a quality God can use for His glory. We all have an ingredient that can be used to bring other people to Christ. If you have a hobby, use it for God. If you have a talent, bring Christ into it and let God have the glory. If you're a photographer, capture the essence of life God has created. If you're a writer, let the spirit use you to write about how good God is right here and right now. If you're in marketing, make Christ the product and watch it flourish. See, we're using the wrong tactics in our lives to gain success and prosperity. We're using techniques of the world, when all we need is Jesus. When you're a child of God and truly allow God to order your steps, then you'll get what you want, when you want it. It's when your steps are being ordered by flesh or man or woman that we all fall short. Oh, if you would only give it all to Christ. If would you only follow the path to righteousness and holiness, God will set everything in order. God is the high commander and when you surrender and enlist in His army, He will organize your life into its own small slice of heaven.

You see, heaven is meant to be experienced right here and right now. However, because we put everything between God and us, it's hard to experience the promised life. Therefore, we must put away those things that drive a wedge between God and us. Remember, He's a jealous God who wants us all to Himself. He doesn't want to share us with anything or anybody. He wants us 100% dedicated and devoted to Him because if we remain in Him and He remains in us, then we will produce good fruit. This means if we totally sell out for Him, then He will remain in us (Holy Spirit) and we will reap the harvest of blessings, good health, prosperity and an abundant life. Therefore, continue to read your word, let God search your heart and remove those things that separate you from His love. Then give Him your all, obedience, prayer and sacrifice. For all these things will keep you in His good graces and He will give you the desires of your heart.

Heavenly Father, open the floodgates of heaven and give me the desires of my heart, after you have searched for a blemish. Should there be a blemish Father, I ask you to forgive me and receive my prayers unto you, for I seek to please you and you alone. Hear my prayer, in the name of Jesus. Amen.

Word of the Day – Continue!

Ruth 2:13
"May I **continue** to find favor in your eyes, my lord,"
she said. "You have given me comfort and have
spoken kindly to your servant—though I do not have
the standing of one of your servant girls."

1 Samuel 3:21
"The LORD **continue**d to appear at Shiloh, and there
he revealed himself to Samuel through his word."

2 Samuel 7:29
"Now be pleased to bless the house of your servant,
that it may **continue** forever in your sight; for you, O
Sovereign LORD, have spoken, and with your
blessing the house of your servant will be blessed
forever."

Psalm 100:5
"For the LORD is good and his love endures forever;
his faithfulness **continue**s through all generations."

This morning I was awakened by a faint voice in the
distance calling for my help. It was my mother slipping
into diabetic shock. Her glucose level had dropped to
62, her speech was slurred, and she could not walk. I
was a nervous wreck. I didn't know how to check her
sugar and was running around the house like a mad
woman, then I stopped and did the only thing I knew
how – Pray. I then got my healing oil and prayed
some more. I continued to call on the name of Jesus,
while rubbing her from head to toe. You see I
recognized the attack of the enemy because he
doesn't want healing and deliverance to take place.
He doesn't want us to have a testimony about the
goodness of the Lord. That's why we must continue to

praise God, in season and out of season. We must continue to call on His name whether we're feeling down or feeling up. We must continue to delight ourselves in His Word. For the Word and God are one. They are dependent of each other. The Word brings life to the soul and spirit because God is life. The Word brings deliverance because God is a deliver. The Word brings healing because God is a healer. The Word brings restoration because God is a restorer.

Just in dealing with my mothers' sickness, I know I have to continue to remain 100% in the hands of the Lord because only He can bring me through this test and these attacks. Only He can love me and care for me when the lights are out and I'm all alone. I have to continue to seek Him with all my heart, while He can still be found, for no man knows the day nor the hour of Christ return. I have to continue to get my soul together, for His word says, "that He might sanctify and cleanse her with the washing of water by the word, that He might present her to Himself a glorious church, not having spot or wrinkle or any such thing, but that she should be holy and without blemish." - Ephesians 5:26-27. What does this scripture mean? It means we are the glorious church Christ is coming back for without a spot or wrinkle but holy. Therefore, some us need to search our personal sanctuary with the eyes of Christ and put away those things separating us from the glory of God. Thus allowing the word of God to wash us and sanctify us before the day of rapture.

We must continue to seek Him until the spirit of God transforms us into the image of Christ. We must continue to walk in His ways until the plans of God manifest in our lives. We must continue to seek righteousness until we are walking in an upright position before the Lord. For what you think, no one else sees, the Lord sees. He is the alpha and the omega. He gives life and He takes life. That's what makes Him the All Mighty One. If you don't have the fear of God in you, then you're continuing on the path of sin and self. For those who truly fear the Lord keep His commandments and seek Him out of respect and fear.

Dear Lord, as I continue on this path to Christ hold my hands and watch my steps. Keep your hand of favor upon me and keep the enemy at bay, so that I shall not grieve in my spirit from his attacks. In the name of Jesus, I lift this prayer up to you. Amen.

Word of the Day – Morning!

Exodus 16:12
"I have heard the grumbling of the Israelites. Tell them, 'At twilight you will eat meat, and in the **morning** you will be filled with bread. Then you will know that I am the LORD your God.' "

Exodus 34:2
"Be ready in the **morning**, and then come up on Mount Sinai. Present yourself to me there on top of the mountain."

1 Samuel 1:19
"Early the next **morning** they arose and worshiped before the LORD and then went back to their home at Ramah. Elkanah lay with Hannah his wife, and the LORD remembered her."

1 Chronicles 23:30
"They were also to stand every **morning** to thank and praise the LORD. They were to do the same in the evening"

Sometimes I'm awakened early in the morning by a feeling that it's time to get up. At first, I didn't understand why I would just awaken and lie there. Then I realized that God wanted to speak to me. He wanted to reveal things to me that He couldn't do in the midst of noise and distractions. He wanted to speak to my spirit man. He wanted to have a conversation with my mind. He wanted to shape my heart. God is never in the middle of confusion. He's a man of order. Although He's a powerful man, He's a man of meekness. He wants to speak to us under the morning dew, which is at His highest glory. There's something about those early morning conversations.

There's power in waking up at 5 a.m. and getting down on your knees in prayer. There's wisdom in letting God minister to your spirit at 4 a.m. There's knowledge in reading your word at 6 a.m. before you go to work. God never sleeps and He operates at our best in the midst of the calmness of daybreak.

Morning manna kept the Israelites fed in the desert. To the Israelites, the manna was bread but for us the manna is the word of God. It's in the early morning that you can have God's full attention. The wee hours attract the ears of God and He hears your prayer. It isn't that He doesn't hear them any other time but there's something special about the wee morning hours. For when you sacrifice your time and get up extra early, it shows God that you are truly seeking Him. It's when you don't care that you only slept for 2 hours that you demonstrate that you want all of God at any cost. God loves us to sacrifice. He loves us to sacrifice our time, our meals, and our finances. It's in the sacrifice that God sees our strengths and weaknesses. It's in the sacrifice that He sees the areas that need to be built up or torn down. For God knows how to bring a person down to his/her knees.

So, if you're not a morning person become one. Ask God to wake you up in the morning and show you visions or whisper in your ear. Get up in the morning and read your bible, asking God to give you revelations. When you wake up in the morning; thank God for your life, health and strength. Give Him all the glory, love and respect a man of his caliber deserves. Late in the midnight hours, speak your hearts desire then in the early morning dew listen for Gods response. For whether He grants your request or denies it, He's still God. Whether you are blessed right away or later down the road, He's still Jehovah.

It doesn't matter what the outcome is when you know that God is working things out for the good of those who trust in Him.

Dear Lord, reveal yourself to me. Reveal your splendor, your glory and your plans for my life. I have a made up mind to live right for you and I want you to speak to me and show me the path you have for my life. Forgive me of any sin that I have put before you and receive my prayer into your heart. In the name of Jesus, amen.

Word of the Day – Sweet!

Judges 14:18
"Before sunset on the seventh day the men of the town said to him, "What is **sweet**er than honey? What is stronger than a lion?" Samson said to them, "If you had not plowed with my heifer, you would not have solved my riddle.""

Psalm 19:10
"They are more precious than gold, than much pure gold; they are **sweet**er than honey, than honey from the comb."

Psalm 119:103
"How **sweet** are your words to my taste, sweeter than honey to my mouth!"

Proverbs 13:19
"A longing fulfilled is **sweet** to the soul, but fools detest turning from evil."

The Lord is sweet. His promises are sweet. His blessings are sweet. His love is sweet. His mercy is sweet. His forgiveness is sweet. Yes, everything about Him is sweeter than honey from the comb. He's magnificent. He's the All Mighty One. He's Jehovah. He's El Shaddai. He's Elohim. He's all that and a bag of chips, with some dip on the side. As you can tell, I'm in total love with my God. How could I not love Him? He provides me with my every need. He blesses me from the crown of my head to the very tips of my toes. He cares for me. He warns me of any danger or uncomfortable situations. He's worried about me. He wants to keep me to Himself. He's afraid of letting go because He thinks I'm just a baby, not ready for the pasture. Yet, as I gain my walking legs, I continue to lean on Him instead of letting Him carry me all the way and all the time. Yes, He's overprotective like any good father.

You know fathers love their daughters. Daughters are the apples of their eyes. Every father thinks his daughter is sweet, even when she might not be. They think they are the best, even when their little girl falls short. I've done a lot of things to a lot of people and with a lot of people, but He still thinks I'm His sweet little girl. He surprises me with gifts of affection and blesses me with promises of a better life. It's because I turned away from my evil traits. It's because He loves me so much that I try to teach others the way to the Father, which is through Jesus. For Jesus Christ is the light, the way, the truth and the only way to the Father. No one gets to the Father except through Him. This is why you must have a personal relationship with Jesus. You must understand Jesus role in your life.

Christmas is about reminding us why the Messiah was born. He was born that we might have life and life more abundantly. He walked this earth teaching, healing and delivering those in bondage. He taught that the kingdom of heaven is at hand. Meaning it's right here. You can enjoy heaven right here and right now, if we all only turn away from our evil ways and embrace a Christ like life. How sweet would the world be with us all on one accord? How sweet would life be with everyone saying, God bless you and really meaning it? How sweet would your home be if everyone praised God with all their heart and wanted no part of any malice or mischief? It would be sweeter than honey. In fact, it would be a thick glaze peace in the air.

Some have missed the sweet life, while others are sitting on there's because of fear or lack of knowledge. While yet others don't know how to get there but are searching for it. It's right there at your fingers tips, but it requires one thing. Jesus! Jesus is the sweet life. He's the road to salvation, freedom, and the Kingdom. You've missed out on a lot of things in your life. Now I beseech you, don't miss out on Jesus. It's a mistake that will haunt you forever.

Heavenly Father, you are a sweet savior to my soul. You name dances in my heart and sings to my spirit. I love you with all my heart and I am growing in your ways. Please continue the good work that is growing my life. In the name of Jesus, amen.

List the ways you've been hurt in the past:

_____
_____
_____
_____
_____
_____
_____
_____
_____
_____

List how you will allow God to heal past hurts:

_____
_____
_____
_____
_____
_____
_____
_____
_____
_____

Dear Heavenly Father, I put my life in the palms of your hands. Mold me and shape me as you please. I'm clay on the potter's wheel and you're the potter. Shape me into the person you're calling me to become. Open the doors and make straight the way of your complete will in my life that it may be done on earth as it is in heaven.

I seek to be blameless before you, clean me up and dust me off. Order my every step that I may walk with you into your promises. You are my Lord and Savior, it's in you I have my hope. Hear my call and incline your ear unto your servant, who's called by your name. My life depends only on you and to you belong all the glory on earth. Thank you, Jesus. Amen.

Word of the Day – Doubt!

Matthew 14:31
"Immediately Jesus reached out his hand and caught him. "You of little faith," he said, "why did you **doubt**?"

Matthew 21:21
"Jesus replied, "I tell you the truth, if you have faith and do not **doubt**, not only can you do what was done to the fig tree, but also you can say to this mountain, 'Go, throw yourself into the sea,' and it will be done."

Luke 24:38
"He said to them, "Why are you troubled, and why do **doubt**s rise in your minds?""

John 20:27
"Then he said to Thomas, "Put your finger here; see my hands. Reach out your hand and put it into my side. Stop **doubt**ing and believe.""

There's a song that we sing in our church and I woke up with it in my spirit, humming it all the way to work. It goes like this:

This morning when I rose up,
I didn't have no doubt
Because the Lord,
He'll take care of me
Because the Lord,
He'll provide for me
Because the Lord,
He will guide me all the way, all the way…

Yes, this morning when I rose up, I didn't have no doubt that the Lord was going to care, protect and guide me all the way. Moreover, this is not only for me but also for my entire family. I have no doubt that God is who He says He is. I have no doubt that He is the "I AM" of Moses. I have no doubt that He is the "Lord of Host" of David. I have no doubt that He's Jehovah Rafah, "HEALER" of Israel. I don't doubt His presence nor power. For I know that the Lord of Host is the Lord strong and mighty. I know "I AM" is the Lord of all. I know "I AM" is the beginning and the end. There's not a doubting bone in me. I know and love the Lord of my soul.

He's the Lord of my heart. He's the Lord of my mind. He's the Lord of my spirit. He's the Lord of my home, my life, daughter, mother, sister, ministry, body, finances, health, prosperity, my whole being. Yes, He's all that. Yes, I've made Him into my life support. Why? Well, I finally realized that if I truly make the Lord into everything I ever wanted, needed or hoped for then He would manifest Himself and prevail in my life.

If this sounds crazy, then you haven't been reading your bible. If you think I'm crazy then you don't know Jesus. For Jesus is the ultimate example of a person that was a seeker of the Lord and He wanted for nothing, then took it even further and laid down His life to save those in bondage and darkness. This brings me to these questions. What have you sacrificed for the Lord? Whom have you saved besides yourself? To love God means to surrender and let Him clean you up. Once you're clean, you must help those in need see the light, thus saving them from a life of destruction. Therefore, since I am allowing God to work in my life I have no doubt that I'm on the right path. I have no doubt that He wants to reward me for my sacrifices and commitment to being His servant. I have no doubt that He will show up

when I need Him to show up. I have no doubt that
He's heard my prayers and ready to answer them. I
have no doubt that He is who He says He is. Do you
have any doubts?

*Dear Lord, I have no doubt that you are working in my
life and that you are working things out to my good.
You are a merciful Lord that I trust all the way. I thank
you for your love and faithfulness in my love. In
Jesus name, I pray. Amen.*

Word of the Day – Set Time!

Genesis 17:21
"But My covenant I will establish with Isaac, whom Sarah shall bear to you at this **set time** next year."

Exodus 9:5
"Then the LORD appointed a **set time**, saying, "Tomorrow the LORD will do this thing in the land."

Job 14:13
"Oh, that You would hide me in the grave, That You would conceal me until Your wrath is past, That You would appoint me a **set time**, and remember me!"

Psalm 102:13
"You will arise and have mercy on Zion; For the time to favor her, Yes, the **set time**, has come."

There's a set time for everything in the eyes of the Lord. For His timing is not our timing, nor His ways neither our ways, nor His plans our plans, yet they all may come together at the end. The Lord knows the desires of our heart and He seeks to meet every need and every want. His word says that, He will not hold back any good thing. However, there's a set time for everything. Ecclesiastes 3:1-8 speaks of timing:

There is a time for everything,
and a season for every activity under heaven:
A time to be born and a time to die,
A time to plant and a time to uproot,
A time to kill and a time to heal,
A time to tear down and a time to build,
A time to weep and a time to laugh,
A time to mourn and a time to dance,
A time to scatter stones and a time to gather them,

A time to embrace and a time to refrain,
A time to search and a time to give up,
A time to keep and a time to throw away,
A time to tear and a time to mend,
A time to be silent and a time to speak,
A time to love and a time to hate,
A time for war and a time for peace.

Now is the set time to rejoice in all this things that the sweet Lord has done for you this year. Now is the set time to uplift your hands and voice unto the Lord with thanksgiving on your tongue and in your spirit. Now is the set time to do your victory dance for the enemy is under your feet. Now is the set time to look back at where God has brought you from and scream, "Thank you Jesus". Now is the set time to let all the haters now that favor has fallen on you. Now is the set time to complete that project. Now is the set time to sing your song. Now is the set time to buy that house. Now is the set time to move on to brighter things. Now is the set time to take that new job. Now is the set time to step out on faith. Now is the set time to praise the Lord. Now is the set time to buy that new car. Now is the set time to take back what the enemy stole from you. Now is the set time to lose those 50lbs. Now is the set time to put God first and everything else behind. Now is the set time to worship at his feet. Now is the set time to discard all the baggage that was holding you down. Now is the set time to be that bride. Now is the set time to be that groom. Now is the set time to birth that child. Now is the set time to be all you can be in Christ Jesus. Now is the set time to let the Holy Spirit light your soul on fire. Now is the set time to put down all things that are separating you from the glory of God. Now is the set time to be blessed. Now is the set time for favor. Now is the set time for health. Now is the set time for prosperity. Now is the set time God's best.

I want to speak life into everyone's life that reads this document. I want you to not only hear the word of God but be doers of the word. Step out on faith and do what's in your heart. Step out on faith and let God know that you trust Him 100%. Give from your heart and God will give from his heart. Therefore, stop being cheap, so that God doesn't have to give you cheap blessings. Love with all your might, as Christ loves the Church. Set time aside for fasting and praying and God will manifest Himself in the process through visions, dreams and prophecy. Seize the moment and let God take you to a higher level, for God has a miracle for you. This is the set time!

Thank you, Lord, for this season of increase and miracles. Thank you for placing me on higher ground and using me. This is the set time for me to step out on faith and depend on you. Don't let me fall, Father, in the name of Jesus. Amen.

Word of the Day – Enlarge!

1 Chronicles 4:10
"Jabez cried out to the God of Israel, "Oh, that you would bless me and **enlarge** my territory! Let your hand be with me, and keep me from harm so that I will be free from pain." And God granted his request."

Exodus 34:24
"I will drive out nations before you and **enlarge** your territory, and no one will covet your land when you go up three times each year to appear before the LORD your God."

Isaiah 26:15
"You have enlarged the nation, O LORD; you have **enlarged** the nation. You have gained glory for yourself; you have extended all the borders of the land."

2 Corinthians 9:10
"Now he who supplies seed to the sower and bread for food will also supply and increase your store of seed and will **enlarge** the harvest of your righteousness."

Just about every night I pray the prayer of Jabez, which is in 1Chronicles 4:10. I first learned of this prayer from watching a popular stage play. I quickly did some research and came across not only the scripture but also a book on the prayer, which opened my eyes to the blessings of God. The prayer illustrated God increasing the territory of a man named Jabez because he put a request up before Him and God found him honorable. To increase ones territory means to broaden that which seems to have a limit or boundary. Increase my faith. Increase my health. Increase my thinking. Increase my finances. Increase my life span. Increase my love. Increase my giving. Increase my patience. Increase my tolerance. Increase my wisdom. Increase my knowledge. Increase my family. When I go down in prayer, I want God to enlarge everything around me. I want Him to stretch it out, increase it and run it over.

It's nice to be able to get a prayer through. It's nice to know that when you go down in prayer that God hears exactly what you're asking for and grants your request. Some of us don't know that God hears us, let alone whether or not He's going to grant our request. I have been fortunate in getting more than a couple of prayers through. Most of the prayers haven't been for me but for others. This is why I know He'll take care of me when I need a breakthrough. For to pray for someone else is a sacrifice. I'm sacrificing my request to ensure God blesses another. It's honorable before God and makes Him want to bless you even more.

Yes, God is enlarging my territory. In fact, He's enlarging it right now as I type. He's working things out to the good for my sake. He's moving things into place for me to receive an overflow of His mercy. He's in the midst of releasing His glory onto the crown of my head. Why? Because I'm just that crazy to trust in Him all the way. I'm just that fool to depend on Him with my entire life. See I know that as He enlarges, He's tearing down. As the Lord increases, something is being decreased. As He builds up, something is being brought low. The world is made up of checks and balances. That's why we must always check ourselves to make sure we balance out to God's expectations.

Do you want your territory enlarged? If you do, then trust God with all your heart, soul, mind and spirit. Love your neighbor as you love yourself. Put God first in all that you do and He'll make a way for you to prosper and increase whatever you put your hand on. Through His mercy and grace, you are redeemed, thus eligible to be blessed. Ask Him to enlarge you and watch how He works things out.

Thank you, Lord, for working things out to the good of those who trust in you. You are my light and my lifeline. Continue to mentor me, protect me and provide for me, as I continue to call on your holy name. In Jesus precious name, amen.

Word of the Day – Dress!

Luke 12:27
"Consider how the lilies grow. They do not labor or spin. Yet I tell you, not even Solomon in all his splendor was **dressed** like one of these."

Luke 12:35
"Be **dressed** ready for service and keep your lamps burning,"

John 21:18
"Jesus said, "Feed my sheep. I tell you the truth, when you were younger you **dressed** yourself and went where you wanted; but when you are old you will stretch out your hands, and someone else will dress you and lead you where you do not want to go."

Revelation 3:5
"He who overcomes will, like them, be **dressed** in white. I will never blot out his name from the book of life, but will acknowledge his name before my Father and his angels."

Some of us spend every evening or every morning deciding on our attire for the next day. We can't decide whether to where pants or a skirt. We can't decide which shoes will go with that cute outfit or should we wear our hair up or down. However, we never really think of the attire we'll be wearing when this journey called life is over. What's going to be our dress attire when God calls us home? I think it's an important question because this life is temporary. This life is not forever, Adam and Eve ended an eternal natural life back in the book of Genesis. However, Jesus promised us eternal life in heaven through the repentance of our sins, the crucifixion of our flesh, which allows us to put away the old person and take up a new person, through obedience of the laws that govern heaven and the praise of God our Lord.

Through a Christ filled life, you can have life forever. What is a Christ filled life? It's a life of daily praise and worship. It's a life of meditating on the word of God. It's a life of walking in obedience of the commandments and covenant of God. It's a life of always saying "yes" to God and always saying "no" to the flesh. It's a life of suffering, yet going through each trying time trusting in God. It's a life, which begins in the sanctuary with the acceptance of Jesus as your personal Lord and Savior, and a made up mind to serve God.

When I go to work, I try to dress for success. I try to dress to illustrate that I am every bit of what I was hired to perform and much more. I dress in an attire, which indicates I'm going places. When I go to church, I dress to illustrate how good God is to me. He sanctified me. My dress attire shows that I'm serious about worshipping and serving God. However, it's not all in the physical attire but more in the spiritual attire. Spiritually, I'm dressed in holiness, righteousness, sincerity, honesty, love, forgiveness, open-mindedness, and obedience. My spiritual dress is more important than the outside attire. For the white robe I will receive covers the spirit which has been granted eternal life though Christ.

It's because of my determination to be a citizen of heaven that I have turned away from everything wicked and opened my heart to everything of God. I didn't want to spend this journey being blind nor spend eternity in hell. Therefore, if your eyes aren't open then think of all Jesus did on your behalf. Think on His suffering and pain for you and me. Think of the life that He wants you to have for your namesake, and then make up your mind that you want to see heaven. Make up your mind that you want to see the glory of God and give God your best.

Dear Lord, thank you for dressing this sinned filled soul with the salvation of Christ. Thank you for your love and mercy. Thank you for receiving me into your arms as a loving Father. Keep me from the evils of this world as I put all my hope in you. In the name of Jesus, I lift my voice unto you. Amen.

Word of the Day – Forgot!

__Deuteronomy 32:18__
"You deserted the Rock, who fathered you; you
forgot the God who gave you birth."

__Job 11:6__
"and disclose to you the secrets of wisdom, for true
wisdom has two sides. Know this: God has even
forgotten some of your sin."

__Jeremiah 2:32__
"Does a maiden forget her jewelry, a bride her
wedding ornaments? Yet my people have **forgotten**
me, days without number."

__Hosea 13:6__
"When I fed them, they were satisfied; when they
were satisfied, they became proud; then they **forgot**
me."

God is a God of many skills, talents, abilities and
remarkable power. We are His cherished beings,
whom He delights in exposing His character to. He is
holy, righteous, honest, trustworthy and noble. He has
never forgotten anyone of us, nor forgotten any
problem, nor forgot to come through for us when we
we're really backed up in a corner. Not the God we
serve. No, He doesn't forget anything about us. The
word says He cares so much about us that He kept
count of every hair on our head. No, God has not
forgotten.

It's us who quickly forget. We forget where He's
brought us from. How He helped our parents raise us
on one income. How He helped us get jobs. How He
helped us get out of sticky situations. How He follows

us to make sure we're safe and protected. How He loves us when no one else does. How He picks us up when we fall down. How He wipes away the tears when our hearts are broken. How He whispers in our ear to let us know that He's still there.

I thank God for not forgetting me. I thank Him for not forgetting to forgive me of all my iniquities. I thank Him for not forgetting to have mercy on my soul. I thank Him for not forgetting to bless me and my household. I thank Him for the saints of God that hold me up in prayer. I thank Him for every breath that I take, everyday. I thank Him because He surely has not forgotten all the promises that He whispered in my ear.

I know that it's just a matter of time before they are to manifest, for the Lord has not forgotten. When it's my season, the promises will arise and God will have all the Glory. For He is worthy to be praise, not because He has blessed me but because He is an awesome God.

What do you thank God for or have you forgotten?

Dear Lord, I thank you for my past, present and future. I thank you for not forgetting me even when I was down in Lo-debar. I thank you for picking me up, dusting me off and planting my feet on solid ground. Now teach me heavenly Father, how to live for you, for my life isn't the same, now that I have you. In the name of Jesus, hear me Lord. Amen.

Word of the Day – Fixed!

Psalm 91:1
"HE WHO dwells in the secret place of the Most High shall remain stable and **fixed** under the shadow of the Almighty [Whose power no foe can withstand]."

Psalm 108:1
"O God, my heart is **fixed**; I will sing and give praise, even with my glory."

Psalm 112:7
"He shall not be afraid of evil tidings: his heart is **fixed**, trusting in the LORD."

Psalm 141:8
"But my eyes are **fixed** on you, O Sovereign LORD; in you I take refuge—do not give me over to death."

My eyes are fixed on the ways of God. Despite what anyone else says or thinks, I must walk as my Lord and Savior dictates. It is written in the book of life, which we call the bible that we must serve, obey, worship and praise the living God. He alone is the author of our destiny and fate. There's not one word in the bible that should be discredited, no matter how things have changed, for God is still the same. As He was during the Old Testament, He was during the New Testament and He's the same God today. His requirements for eternal life have not changed, nor His terms for death. For the wages of sin is death but the wages for holiness is eternal life. Not just in heaven but right here, in this place we call earth.

His requirements to be blessed have not changed. This fixed formula began as early as Adam and Eve. Although, they sinned and thus contaminated the ingredients, the formula is still the same. Just like, we have fixed interest rates, which we can lock into so that regardless of the change in the economy our rate stays the same. We also have the power of God that we can lock into; a fixed trinity. There's nothing about Gods' ways, personality or character that changes. Our environment might change, our location might change, our destination might change, we might change our minds, our intentions might change but the God that we're locked into doesn't change. The outcome through God doesn't change. It's the same each and every time, victorious.

Although, Gods' personality doesn't change, His plans may. Yes, God can flip the script. Yes, God can change His mind and do things differently. Well, that's the way it seems to us at least because we think we know God and the path He has us on. However, some of us will never fully know the details of our life in Christ. I think that's because we think to small, when God has no limitations. We think inside the box when God is outside, on the left, on the right, straight ahead and never looking back. Many of us don't think and believe in the impossible. However, if you truly fix your heart, spirit and mind on all the full power of God and step into a higher level of praise, then you will know that there's nothing impossible for God; for He performs exceedingly abundantly above all things.

With God, there's no such thing as fixed assets, because He wants to triple them. There's no such thing as fixed interest on your banking account, because He wants to double it. There's no such thing as a fixed health condition because He wants to bring you out.

Therefore, fix your eyes upon the Lord and He will fix His ear upon your request. Stay focused despite everything around you. For this walk is between you and God, and no one else.

Lord, I thank you for every area of my life that you have fixed. I thank you for fixing my brokenness, I thank you for fixing my corruptness and I thank you for fixing my emptiness. You are a merciful savior that is just indeed. In the name of Jesus, I pray that you continue fixing that which needs repair in my life. Amen.

Word of the Day – Living Water!

Jeremiah 17:13
"O LORD, the hope of Israel, all who forsake you will be put to shame. Those who turn away from you will be written in the dust because they have forsaken the LORD, the spring of **living water**."

John 4:10
"Jesus answered her, "If you knew the gift of God and who it is that asks you for a drink, you would have asked him and he would have given you **living water**."

John 7:38
"Whoever believes in me, as the Scripture has said, streams of **living water** will flow from within him."

Revelation 7:17
"For the Lamb at the center of the throne will be their shepherd; he will lead them to springs of **living water**. And God will wipe away every tear from their eyes."

Jesus said He will give us living water. What is living water? The living water is Jesus. The living water is the Holy Spirit. The living water is the word of God. Jesus, the Holy Spirit and the word are living water for your soul, your mind and for your spirit. This water is living and active. It accomplishes changes and transformations in who ever takes hold of it. For in the water of Christ is the seal of life. You see the living water holds more than just nutrients. The living water is that which enters us from God and penetrates every empty and corruptible area of our soul. It holds healing power, salvation, the anointing, it's the blood of Jesus, it's freedom, it's wealth, it's prosperity, it's long life, it's the purpose of God. The living water of

God cleanses out the old person, the corrupt things, the despicable elements, the ungodly things, the unrighteousness and makes a new creature. It's like purifying gold. The process may be painful but the craftsman is patient, gentle, caring, loving, and merciful and a perfectionist.

Once you're in the hands of God, all things are made new again. All things are made alive again, joy is restored, inner peace is renewed, all childish things are put away, all ungodly things removed, and you become a new holy servant of the Lord. That's if you want to serve the Lord with all your heart. That's if you desire to worship Him in your most naked state. See the God we serve doesn't force us to do anything against our will. He will only come into our lives and clean us up if we want Him to come in. He'll only show us His salvation if we want to be free from bondage. He'll only pour Himself out to us if we surrender to our inner thirst for a closer relationship with God. It's once we acknowledge our thirst that He says, He's the living water we've been looking for all along.

I once had a thirst for fornication. It occupied my every thought and every handsome man in eyesight made me tingle. Then one day I got a hold of some living water. This living water was the word of God, it was the truth, and it was the fact that the wages of sin is death. I realized I was hell bound because I was outside of the commandments of God and hadn't repented with a sincere heart. Instead, I would repent then fornicate, repent and fornicate, which began a vicious cycle. I was hell bound and didn't know it until the living water activated in my soul and told me that I had to get out of the situation. I turned to God and surrendered completely this time and I never looked back. For to look back means to regret and I have no regrets that I ended a dead relationship with a man to have eternal life with the King.

Therefore, I urge everyone that has a thirst for something more, a thirst for joy, happiness, love, and peace of mind, to go to the source of living water. Who's the source? Jehovah!

Jehovah, please quench my thirst for your resources. Quench my heart for your love. Quench this emptiness and fill me up with your spirit. There's no one like the Lord. There's no one that can stand up against you. In the name of Jesus, please continue to be there for me as I continue to seek you. Amen.

Word of the Day – Power!

Exodus 9:16
"But I have raised you up [Or have spared you] for this very purpose, that I might show you my **power** and that my name might be proclaimed in all the earth."

Exodus 15:6
"Your right hand, O LORD, was majestic in **power**. Your right hand, O LORD, shattered the enemy."

Deuteronomy 8:17-18
"You may say to yourself, "My **power** and the strength of my hands have produced this wealth for me." But remember the LORD your God, for it is he who gives you the ability to produce wealth, and so confirms his covenant, which he swore to your forefathers, as it is today."

Greater is He that is in me, which is Christ Jesus. God is within us; therefore, we have the very same power as Christ Jesus. Power to resist the enemy, power to live a holy life, power to praise Him every day, Holy Ghost power, healing power, power to stand the test and trials that may come our way. If you don't have any power to withstand the attacks of the adversary or withstand your flesh then stretch out on God and ask Him to strengthen you where you're weak. If you don't have the Holy Spirit, ask for it and you shall have it like the Day of Pentecost-Acts 2:4. If you don't have the power to stop fornicating, then ask God to remove your thirst for sex, which is sometimes a cry for love and affection. Ask Him to fill in every empty space that's causing you to crave love in the wrong ways. If your weakness is food, then ask God to give you a taste for the Word. Ask Him to give you a hunger for the bible, and then fill up on it each and every day. If your weakness is lies, then ask God of give you the spirit of truth. Every area you're weak in; seek God to strengthen you in that area. Come clean with God and put everything on the table for evaluation. God wants you to love Him enough to trust Him with your entire life, knowing He has the power to care for you in ways no one else can. Know that only He is able to keep you holy, righteous, sane, healthy, and in perfect peace. Remember that God has the power and authority to make any weakness, imperfection, character flaw, disease; ache, pain and situation disappear and never surface again. However, you have to have faith that God is who He says He is. You have to believe strongly that God is a healer of all things, not just some or a few. You have to know in your heart, mind and soul that there's no limit to the power of God and if He says He's done something or going to do it then it's complete.

This word is blessed because I have made a conscious decision to praise God all the days of my life. This is a decision that you'll have to make on your own. It's a decision to praise Him whether He shows you some of His power, all of His power or none at all.

Dear Lord, I know that there's power in your name. I know that in the name of Jesus, demons have to flee and spirits have to deteriorate because there's power in that name. Your name is superior above all things, which is why I call on you every chance I get. You are my protector, my rescuer and my defender. Never leave me, Lord, for I depend on you. Thank you. Jesus. Amen.

Word of the Day – Against!

Deuteronomy 28:7
"The LORD will grant that the enemies who rise up **against** you will be defeated before you. They will come at you from one direction but flee from you in seven."

Deuteronomy 33:11
"Bless all his skills, O LORD, and be pleased with the work of his hands. Smite the loins of those who rise up **against** him; strike his foes till they rise no more."

Joshua 1:5
"No one will be able to stand up **against** you all the days of your life. As I was with Moses, so I will be with you; I will never leave you nor forsake you."

Mark 9:40
"for whoever is not **against** us is for us."

For we fight not against flesh and bones but against the powers of this dark world. Yes, the world is full of evil powers and evil spirits. These powers seek to suck life out of everything it meets. That's why as Christians, we must continue to wear our full armor. God has given us armor once we became bold soldiers for the Lord. This armor is not that of natural soldier attire, it's neither guns nor grenades. Our armor is the belt of truth, the breastplate of righteousness, the gospel of peace, the shield of faith, the helmet of salvation and the sword of the Spirit, which is the word of God. As Christians, we must equip ourselves each and every day with our essential equipment. This is how we overcome the enemy and dodge his fiery arrows. For the adversary seeks to overthrow our faith, overthrow our commitment to God, overthrow our salvation and any healing we have faith in.

We must remember that anyone that is not saved and working for the good of God and the Kingdom is against the Lord. Although, they may be against God it's our job to bring them to the light and the full knowledge of Christ. We must help them switch sides and fight against the very entity that had them in bondage. Helping them switch sides is not only for the good of the Kingdom but also for the good of their soul. For no man knows the very minute, hour, nor day of the return of Christ. It's going to take all of us by surprise and most importantly, the saints. For the saints know the bible and should know by now the do's and the don'ts.

- Do love God with all your heart, all your soul, your entire mind and all your spirit.
- Do love your neighbor as you love yourself.
- Do trust God with your entire life, possessions, assets and family.
- Don't curse God, for He will curse you in return.
- Don't disobey God's commandants or covenant.
- Don't put anything before God. He is first over everything.

These few guidelines are important because if you follow just the few then you're showing that you're for God. If you just begin to love Him with your entire being then you're welcoming Him into you life, thus working against the evil powers of this world. If you start laying everything aside and truly focus on serving God and honoring Him in your life daily, then you're working for the goodness of the Kingdom.

I know it's hard to do all of these guidelines at once. Therefore, take it slow and start by calling on Jesus everyday to come into your life. Then start reading the requirements for heaven, beginning with the New Testament and the life of Jesus. Allow the bible to speak to your heart and work in your spirit. For God only wants us to be citizens of the Kingdom of Heaven. He doesn't want to be against us, He wants to be for us. He wants to bless us, care for us and say, "well done" at the end of it all. Nevertheless, He gives us the choice to choose either for or against the Kingdom. Which one are you choosing?

Lord, though I have some struggles, I pray that you do not hold them against me. Receive my prayers unto your holy ears and help me in all times of trouble. Have mercy on my heart, mind, soul and spirit. Send your grace, so that your strength shall be made perfect through my weakness. In the name of Jesus, amen.

Word of the Day – Fresh!

Job 29:20
"My glory is **fresh** within me, And my bow is renewed in my hand."

Psalm 92:10
"But my horn You have exalted like a wild ox; I have been anointed with **fresh** oil."

Psalm 92:14
"They shall still bear fruit in old age; They shall be **fresh** and flourishing,"

James 3:11
"Does a spring send forth **fresh** water and bitter from the same opening?"

As I welcomed the calling of God in my life, I ask the Lord for a fresh anointing, a fresh revelation of His word and a fresh outlook on how to remain sanctified. Yes, it's hard to remain holy, sanctified and free of sin. Some people aren't honest about their walk with Christ but I have to be honest for the sake of those that want salvation and are not sure how to obtain it and for those who want to remain under the covenant of God. This is a hard walk; don't let anyone fool you into thinking it's a piece of cake. I can't stress the importance of fasting and praying because those are the key factors for remaining close to God.

The number one key is repentance. Repentance has to be a daily part of your spiritual diet. I don't care if you think you don't do any wrong. I don't care how you've perfected your walk with Christ. I don't care if you avoid certain people and places. I don't care how long you've been a Christian; you have to repent on a daily basis.   In fact, the longer you've been a Christian, the more you need to repent. Repent from sun up to sun down. Jesus said, "Repent, for the kingdom of heaven is near" (Matthew 3:2).

King David sinned with Bathsheba and tried to cover it up with murder but he didn't lose his anointing because he repented.   However, sin had an irrevocable effect on his life and family but God remained with King David to the end. All sin has consequences.   You might not see it now but somewhere down the road, it will rear its ugly head. Some of us see our children going through the same issues we went through as young adults.   Why? Because the same sinful spirit continues to torment the next generation, which is why you have to curse all sin from the root. How do you do that? You call it out in prayer and ask God to take it from you and your family.   Fast to purge it from your flesh and give it over to God completely.   Pray over your family rebuking those spirits and binding it up from appearing ever again.

That's what I had to do with my daughter. She was having a difficult time at school and it was everyone's fault but hers. As I laid in prayer, the spirit told me what was tormenting her: jealousy, stubbornness, rejection, loneliness and need for acceptance. In the name of Jesus, I commanded those spirits, those feelings, and demons to unloose her and afflicted her no longer.   I then sent her on her way to school with a fresh start, trusting deliverance took place and there would be no more problems. I had to attack this thing at the root, so fresh seeds could be planted, thus producing a new crop of joy, happiness, love, understanding, and a new sweet spirit.

Now I know the devil is going to come another way, because he can't use that vessel to unleash his rage. Especially since, I intend to fill my daughter with the word of God, thus providing her with salvation instead of self-destruction. Oh, I know the devil is mad and wants to sift me like wheat but I've got on my breastplate, helmet, belt, and I'm always reaching for my sword. For this battle is not against flesh and blood but against powers, principalities, rulers and authorities in heavenly realms. The Apostle Paul urged us to stand and when you feel like you're going to be defeated, stand some more with the full Armor of God (Ephesians 6:14-17) as your weaponry.

Dear Lord, send me a fresh anointing to overcome the attacks of the enemy. Place your hands of protection around me and my family. Continue to dwell in me, Lord, as I remain your faithful child. In Jesus name, amen!

Word of the Day – Anointing!

Exodus 40:9
"Take the anointing oil and **anoint** the tabernacle and everything in it; consecrate it and all its furnishings, and it will be holy."

Isaiah 10:27
"It shall come to pass in that day That his burden will be taken away from your shoulder, And his yoke from your neck, And the yoke will be destroyed because of the **anointing** oil."

1 John 2:20
"But you have an **anointing** from the Holy One, and all of you know the truth."

1 John 2:27
"As for you, the **anointing** you received from him remains in you, and you do not need anyone to teach you. But as his anointing teaches you about all things and as that **anointing** is real, not counterfeit—just as it has taught you, remain in him."

The anointing is a gift from God that must not be rejected, neglected nor abused. The anointing separates you from all the rest of the sheep in the flock. Few have it, many want and some fake it. The anointing holds power, for without the anointing I'm just an ordinary woman, doing ordinary things, speaking ordinary words, but with the anointing, I'm on fire for Christ. The truth is made known through the anointing, thus feeding the spirit things unknown to man. The anointing breaks the yokes of the oppressed, depressed and those dead from sin. With the anointing, nothing unclean and unholy can touch me or tear me down. The anointing makes you invincible to those things that are not of God. The Prophet Jeremiah described it by saying "it's like fire shut up in his bones" (Jeremiah 20:9). As you increase your anointing through studying the word of God, the truth becomes like fire shut up in your bones.

For when the anointing falls on me, I can't help but to be a bold soldier for Christ. I begin to shout, I begin to loose and bind. I begin to command things into existence. I begin to cast things out of my way. I begin to speak life over myself, my situation and those around me. The anointing is a comforting, yet electrifying feeling because it's the power of God rushing through every vein, in your body. It feels as if; God has taken complete control over me. I can't think straight, my legs are out of control, my spirit is on fire and I'm telling it like it is. I'm letting the truth out, which is the word of God. I'm not holding anything back because God doesn't care about your feelings, He only cares about results. He doesn't care if you get mad; He wants you to get delivered. He doesn't care if you walk out; take your bad attitude with you because He comes to bring life and life more abundantly. If you don't want the blessings of God, I'll take your share. Yes, I want all that God has for me and if you don't want yours I'll take those too. Yes, I'm just that bold because I love the anointing. I love the feeling of being able to conquer that which has come to inflict me and rip me apart. I love walking in the full authority of Christ.

I'm an ambassador. I'm royalty. From now on, I'm going to put on my crown every morning when I get up. What's my crown? The anointing is my crown of glory; which is like an over coat being thrown upon my shoulders. How am I going to exercise my anointing?

Through fasting and praying. By allowing God to have complete control over my life, thus sacrificing my will for His and by being obedient to His word and holding dear to His commandants.

The best part about the anointing is that no one can take it away; I have to give it up. That's why I stay on the alter, on my knees in prayer, so this flesh of mine never gets any ideas to exalt itself above all the good work of the Lord.

The anointing is the power that connects me to God. I need it. I depend on it. I can't live without, just like I can't live without God. I need Him. I'm nothing without Him, nor do I have anything without Him. He's everything to me. Make Him everything to you. Your very survival depends on Him. He will protect you. He'll stop the enemies attack. He'll clean you up and place your feet on solid ground, if you lean on Him for your every need. He's a sweet savior, merciful to those who call on His name. Don't stop the anointing. Let it flow from the crown of your head to the sole of your feet.

Dear Lord, may your anointing fall on me today, this very minute, comforting me and imparting all of your heavenly wisdom and knowledge into my spirit. May your power. Dear Lord, manifest in my life, making me a bold soldier for your glory. In Jesus name. Amen!

Word of the Day – Lonely!

Psalm 25:16
"Turn to me and be gracious to me, for I am lonely and afflicted."

Psalm 68:6
"God sets the lonely in families, he leads forth the prisoners with singing; but the rebellious live in a sun-scorched land."

Mark 1:45
"Instead he went out and began to talk freely, spreading the news. As a result, Jesus could no longer enter a town openly but stayed outside in lonely places. Yet the people still came to him from everywhere."

Luke 5:16
"But Jesus often withdrew to lonely places and prayed."

I often look around my house when I'm all alone and feel the spirit of loneliness trying to creep into my soul. My mind then begins to wonder, why God has brought me to this lonely state of life. I don't have friends like I use to, I don't converse like I use to, I don't even laugh like I use to, yet I still have a joy about myself. I'm still optimistic about my future because I've got Jesus in my life as never before.

I've also begun to feel differently in my spirit about the people around me. Last night I received a sad call about a man that came to my church some months ago. I knew him through another friend and he came out to my church when I asked him to hear my first sermon. He came with his grandchildren and we went to church and had dinner together. He was a very nice man, a joy to be around and was on his way back to Christ. In fact, I still remember how he danced down the isles of my church with tears in his eyes. He then went to my pastor for prayer and was on his knees at the altar, receiving salvation. That day was truly miraculous and I'll never forget it. Well, the phone call I received was from a friend, saying the man died of a heart attack. I was in shock. In fact, it brings tears to my eyes right now, just recalling the conversation. It hurts so badly because I don't know whether he was received into the bosom of Christ. I just don't know if he made it in. I don't know if he maintained his salvation and turned away from his old life and embraced the new through the receiving of Christ. I cried aloud last night thinking about this man and the family he left behind. He was returning to Jesus because his sons, the fruits of his seed were turning bad. In fact, one was in jail and I guess the others were following suit and he wanted to change their destinations. He knew if he gave his life to Christ and his children saw God's manifestation in him they would draw closer to God. I truly hope he accomplished what he set out to do, in the name of Jesus.

It just breaks my heart to know that someone is trying to do right; someone is trying to get to Jesus and possibly didn't make it. I know many people say, Jesus knows my heart and that's true. Jesus knows the hearts of all but your heart can love Jesus but your flesh loves to fornicate. Does that mean on the Day of Judgment God will receive you? No. All of your body has to get right. Your heart, your eyes, your legs, mouth, mind, soul and spirit; all of you have to be lined up with Christ.

God is truly changing me because I care so much about other people receiving salvation. I want everyone to be saved. I want everyone to receive Christ and allow Him to change them forever. I know Christ can transform even the lowest, the filthiest person into a beautiful butterfly. The bible is filled with those stories and our churches are filled with those testimonies. Because I care so much and I love so much, I'm asking God to finish the good work He's started in my life. I don't want to die with my works undone. I want to evangelize, I want to preach and teach, heal and set free those held in bondage by the enemy. I don't want to perish with my works still hanging in the air. I don't want to go down to my grave with ideas still in my head. I want to go down knowing I fought a good fight while I was able to command things in the name of Jesus Christ.

Lonely, how could I be lonely when I have so much work to do? How can I be alone when God is with me every second of the day? Lonely, I don't think so. I'm never alone as long as I continue to remain in Christ. Touch yourself and say, "I'm never alone".

Dear Lord, please give me the time I need to accomplish all the works you have before me. Lord, don't let my hands be idle, nor my feet be steady but give me the strength to endure and the resources to accomplish all goals. I pray to you dear Lord, in the name of Jesus. Amen.

Word of the Day – Renew!

Job 29:20
"New honors are constantly bestowed on me, and my strength is continually **renew**ed.'"

Psalm 23:3
"He **renew**s my strength. He guides me along right paths, bringing honor to his name."

Psalm 51:10
"Create in me a clean heart, O God. **Renew** a right spirit within me."

Psalm 94:19
"When doubts filled my mind, your comfort gave me **renew**ed hope and cheer."

Colossians 3:10
"In its place you have clothed yourselves with a brand-new nature that is continually being **renew**ed as you learn more and more about Christ, who created this new nature within you."

Everyday when I arise, I ask God to create in me a clean spirit. Renew my heart, renew my mind, renew my spirit and renew my soul. Often feel I like this world is beating me down. I cry out to God for help, for He is my strength in the times of trouble. He is my counselor in times of worry. He is my savior in times of distress. He renews me like fresh morning dew. He renews me like a rainbow in the sky after a storm has past. He renews me like fresh air on a stale summer day.   He renews my heart from the brokenness of life, men, friends, parents and children.

For in my old age (30'ish), I have learned that God is the only one that loves me despite my attitudes, my fears, my hang-ups, my hang-downs, stubbornness, and my blindness to the path He's trying to pull me on. He has become all I need and all I want and the only person I can depend. He has an answer for everything from, how to raise my daughter to how to do my work on the job. God is my life support.

So, no matter what the problem is, look to God for the answer. Let Him renew your eyesight through Christ to see the resolution of all your worries. Trust in Him and not man or woman. People let people down. I've seen it over and over again but God has a record of success, a solid track record of rescuing those whom trust in Him. He loves the saved, as well as, the unsaved because we are all His children. We all were birthed out of Him.

Anytime I feel myself falling down, I lean to His understanding and trust Him to pick me up. You see, He doesn't think like you or I. No, His rationale is on a higher playing field. He sees things years, decades and generations from now. This is why His plan seems so complex to our feeble minds. Yes, the Lord is awesome in all ways.

Even the way we're conceived is an act of godly brain power. Sometimes I just stare at the way my hands type and the way my feet tap and say, "Wow, God made this". He planned this before I was even in my mothers' womb, He planned for me to break into this world and take it by storm. But because this world can be so cruel, I cling to Him for His help, His love and His mercy. He's got me in the grips of His hands and I can't let go. I'm fearful of falling down, yet afraid to forge ahead.

Dear Lord, create in me a clean spirit and renew my mind, so that I don't faint with fear. I'm keeping my eyes on the prize which is Christ but it seems that I can't live in this world without torment or strife, that's why I need you so, Dear Lord. I need you to keep me from falling down. I need you to hold me up when my legs go weak. I need you to raise my hand, when I don't feel like clapping. I need you all the way and in every way. Be my God, Dear Lord. Be my savior, Heavenly Father. Remain with me, as I continue to remain in you. In Jesus name, amen!

Word of the Day – Joy!

1 Chronicles 16:27
"Splendor and majesty are before him; strength and **joy** in his dwelling place."

Job 8:21
"He will yet fill your mouth with laughter and your lips with shouts of **joy**."

Job 33:26
"He prays to God and finds favor with him, he sees God's face and shouts for **joy**; he is restored by God to his righteous state."

Psalm 16:11
"You have made known to me the path of life; you will fill me with **joy** in your presence, with eternal pleasures at your right hand."

When I think on the goodness of the Lord, one word comes to my mind, "JOY". When I think on the sweet smell of the Lord, one word comes to my mind, "JOY". When I think on how the Lord brought me through all my situations and out into a land of milk and honey, one word comes to me, "JOY". Yes, I've got the love of Jesus and it's sweet joy to my soul.

The Lord is the deliver of all Joy. Some say, He gives joy and He takes it away. However, I say, He gives it and we give it back because we allow others to snatch it out of our hands. Joy is a gift from the Lord and just like any other gift; you can either sit down on it or put it into operation. I know for sure, I'm not going to let anything take my joy away. I worked to hard for it. I went through too much to get it. I fasted too many days, I cried too many nights, I prayed in my home too many afternoons for it. Yes, I've come too far to let my joy slip through my fingers. I watched my mother go through cancer and I kept my joy. I watched my daughter act out in school and I maintained my joy. I went to bed lonely but joy was in my heart. I watched my bank account go up and down but I never let my joy diminish. Yes, joy is just about all I have right now because it's going to see me through.

Some people need gold, yet others need diamonds but I find my wealth in the joy of the Lord because He flips the script and makes dead things alive. My Lord is a healer making the sick recover. My Lord is a savior, stretching out His hand to those in need. My Lord is an accountant making my bills fall in line. My Lord is a realtor, putting homes in my hand. You have to understand where I'm going with this or you'll lose me. God has created everything under the heavens; therefore, it all belongs to Him. The car dealership that says, Bob's, might as well say, Jehovah's. The house for sale by owner, might as well say, Yahweh. The bank, might as well say, Abba because, it all belongs to Him and is under His control.

All we have to do is line up with His calling. All we have to do is follow His instructions and example. All we have to do is crucify flesh and put it under subjection. Thank Him everyday, repent and praise His name. This is not a cliché but a well-known fact, that when the praises go up, the blessings come down. When you praise His name, He opens up the window to find out whose calling. Then, once He recognizes your voice, He looks at your track record. In church every Sunday, prays throughout the day, attends bible study, pays tithes and offerings, obedient to the Holy Spirit, walks when I say walk, runs when I say run, a woman after my own heart, yes, she is. Now that I know who and what I'm dealing with, I'm going to pour out a blessing, so much that you won't have room enough for it (Malachi 3:10b).

It's not only the praises but it's the joy you have with it. It's not only the obedience but the joy you have with it. It's not only the faithfulness but the joy you have with it. Yes, storms are going to come. Situations are going to arise but you don't have to let it take over your joy. Your joy comes directly from God above. He wants us to all be happy, even on the days when it feels like you're not going to make it. That's when I believe He gives you a double-portion of joy; just so you know He's the one that gives you hope to face another day.

Don't be a victim of losing your joy over the mundane things of this world. Tell the devil he's under your feet and he can't steal your joy away because he didn't give it to you, it comes from above.

Dear Heavenly Father, help us face another day of attacks from the enemy with joy. Help us Father, cast Satan under our feet and lean to your understanding that we have the victory through Christ, who suffered for us to have a second chance and a better life. Give us, Lord, the strength to walk in favor and continue to seek your heavenly purpose for our lives. In Jesus name, amen!

Word of the Day –Alive!

1 Samuel 2:6
"The LORD brings death and makes **alive**; he brings down to the grave and raises up."

Ecclesiastes 4:2
"And I declared that the dead, who had already died, are happier than the living, who are still **alive**."

Luke 15:24
"For this son of mine was dead and is **alive** again; he was lost and is found.' So they began to celebrate."

Luke 20:38
"He is not the God of the dead, but of the living, for to him all are **alive**."

Through Christ, we all are alive. Christ is the man-child that came and walked the earth as an everyday man. I think He gave up His authority in heaven temporarily to see just how difficult it actually was for us to present ourselves holy before God and also to be the perfect example of how one can walk in holiness. Yes, I know that He also came to reconcile us back to God, thus make our sins that were once as red as crimson, as white as snow. However, I believe that during His time here, He realized that the many hindrances that seek to interrupt our purity.

Jesus experienced this first-hand when Satan tried tempting Him while fasting for 40 days and 40 nights. Satan tried to deceive Him. He tried to get Him to fall. He tired to get Him to give it all up and forget about us because; after all, we were mere sinners that didn't want to live right.

I thank God that He sent His only begotten son. I thank Jesus for not giving up when Satan turned up the heat. For He could have given in but as the Son of God, He wouldn't. He could have turned His back on us but as a vessel for the Lord, He didn't. He could have cast us to the wind but as our savior, He refused. Through Christ walk, I now know how to stay alive though the devil is trying to kill me. I know how to stay alive when he's feeding poison into my mind. After all, this is a war and the object of any war is to defeat the enemy. How do you defeat the enemy? You defeat him by staying alive. We must all stay alive in our flesh, in our mind, in our spirit and in our faith. We stay alive by keeping our spirits filled with the proper nutrients. With our natural body, we take vitamins, we exercise and we have well balanced meals. With our spiritual body, we live off the word of God, exercise our scriptural knowledge and balance everything out with fasting and much prayer. It's the same routine for both, just different ingredients.

I'm determined to stay alive in this race to Christ. I don't care if I have to drag myself across the finish line, with cuts and scrapes. I don't care If only my finger makes it across the line, it's better than nothing at all. After all, I don't know anything else but living for Christ. I don't know any other race that I'd rather be in, then that of running towards the mark of Christ. Right now, the future of my whole family depends on my relationship with the King.

I'm depending on the King to bring my sisters into this race. I'm trusting the King to water the seed that's been planted in my mother. I'm believing the King to finish the good work started in my father and through him, bring my bothers into this walk. There's generations that are depending on my relationship with Christ, just like there's generations that are depending on your relationship with Christ. This is why it's so important that you keep God alive and active in your life. For it's not only for your sake and your immediate family but generations are depending on you to bring them into the promises of God.

Dear Lord, as I seek your face order my steps in your will. Keep me on the path that you would have me to go. For I seek you not only for myself but for future generations. I'm asking you, dear Lord, to bless my entire household and family. Bless from the first born to the least born, as we seek you and stay in your good graces. In the name of Jesus, I pray. Amen.

Bonus
Word of the Day – Pray!

Genesis 24:12
"Then he **pray**ed, "O LORD, God of my master Abraham, give me success today, and show kindness to my master Abraham."

Deuteronomy 4:7
"What other nation is so great as to have their gods near them the way the LORD our God is near us whenever we **pray** to him?"

Psalm 6:9
"The LORD has heard my cry for mercy; the LORD accepts my **pray**er."

Luke 11:1
"One day Jesus was **pray**ing in a certain place. When he finished, one of his disciples said to Him, "Lord, teach us to **pray**, just as John taught his disciples."

The Lord, strong and mighty, just and righteous hears the prayers of all, that take the time to lift them up to Him. Some people think you have to be in prayer for hours, while other say you only need to make a request once and others say pray without ceasing all throughout the day. I prefer to pray without ceasing all throughout the day because I am at a point in my life where I can't not talk to Him. I can't not call on His name. I can't not think about Him. He's constantly on my mind, in my heart and in my spirit. I owe so much to Him. He's the love of my life. He's the man of my dreams and I can't live without Him in my life, nor go throughout the day without communicating with Him.

I want Him to be involved in every aspect of my life. In order for Him to be involved, I must call on Him. I must get Him involved by providing Him the details. My boss is in town this week from Houston and I'm nervous about the visit. Therefore, what did I do? I went to God when He woke me up at 5 am; I began to ask Him to cover me during this visit. I asked Him to be with me, help me make it through; tell me what to say and how to say it. He's the one that gave me this job and I know that He wants me to keep it until it's time to move on. What God, has provided, no one can take it away but we can give it up. How can we give it up?   We give up God's blessings and provisions by walking in disobedience, allowing sin to enter our lifestyles, not allowing God to control our environment and atmosphere. Not only does He want to be involved in our every decision but He also wants us to follow His instructions. They are instructions, not recommendations. When the instructions on a box say, add 2 parts water to the formula, we do not do the opposite. We follow the instructions to the exact detail, if we want the finished product to come out successful. These are the same precautions we need to take with God's instructions.

I can't stress the importance of surrendering to God. It is vital not only to our Christian walk but our very survival hood depends on us succumbing to the power of Christ. The devils is real and guess what, He has a strategy but if you walk in the spirit and not in flesh, he shall not prevail. That is why it's vital to yield to God all the way. To yield half way, means to produce half of the results. To yield all the way, means to receive all God has for you. I don't know about you but I am greedy. I want it all, everything, and some of yours, if you don't want it. I'm not letting any of it pass me by nor slip through my fingers for any of the silly and minuet stuff that's going on around us.

It's too late in the evening for me to turn back to my old ways. I have to press. In fact, I have no other choice but to press on towards the mark of Christ. I have to do the work of Him that sent me. I have to take the position of Him that birthed me. Souls are dying without salvation. Souls are screaming for help and don't know how to call on Jesus. Souls want out of bondage but don't know whom to turn to and that is where I come in. I've been praying to God, if no one else want to go on the battleground, Lord send me. If no one else wants to fight, I pray, Lord send me. If no one else wants to save them, I pray, Lord prepare me. I don't know where God is taking me on this journey but I pray, higher, Lord, higher, Lord.

There's so much going on around me and it's breaking my heart. I can't stop weeping and I can't stop shaking my head. Our people, dear Lord, are dying from a lack of knowledge. They are dying because they don't know there's a King that can set them free. A King who reigns on the high, just as well as the low. A King who owns everything and will give to those who call on His holy name. A King who can set them free, if they would only set their hearts on Him. This King is Jehovah, Elohim, El Shaddai, Abba, The Lord Almighty, and Christ Jesus. Whichever name you should select to use, call on Him and don't let go until He blesses you.

I called on Him one day and He changed my life. I called on Him one day and He changed my name. I called on Him one day and I've never been the same. Stop sitting and letting this time pass you by. Grab hold to the name of Christ and let Him have His way.

For His way is the only way. Go while the sun is still up and the evening has not set completely.

Dear Lord, as I complete this 31-day devotional in your holy name, I pray that you enlarge my territory with a rich blessing. Come into my life like never before and manifest your presence. I have learned, Lord, that I want to live for you all the way. Fill us up with your precious spirit, so that we will never be the same. Transform us into beautiful butterflies, free, loving and caring. In the name of Jesus, I pray. Amen.

Prayer List
(List the people you're going to call out in prayer)

_____

_____

_____

_____

_____

_____

_____

_____

_____

_____

_____

_____

_____

_____

_____

_____

_____

_____

_____

_____

_____

_____

_____

_____

_____

_____

_____

A Plan for Restoration

1. Go to a church. A church where you can really praise and worship God any way you want to.

2. Confess your sins. This can be done between you and the Lord, if you don't feel comfortable speaking with your pastor.

3. Empty yourself out on the altar. Cry, shout, yell, shake, dance, or sing, whatever it takes. Give god every ache, pain, complaint, whimper, issue, problem, situation and leave it at the altar.

4. Tell God what you want Him to do for you. Tell Him every want, need, special request, hope, and dream. Give Him everything.

5. Continue to go to church and just praise Him.

6. Pray everyday.

7. Watch for results.

Prayer Recipe!
(Pray this nightly)

Praise be to the God and Father of my Lord Jesus Christ, who has blessed me in the heavenly realms with every spiritual blessing in Christ (Ephesians 1:3). Therefore I tell you, whatever I ask for in prayer, I believe that I have received it, and it will be mines (Mark 11:24). For this reason I kneel before the Father, from whom his whole family in heaven and on earth derives its name. I pray that out of your glorious riches you may strengthen me with power through your Spirit in my inner being, so that Christ may dwell in my heart through faith. And I pray that I, being rooted and established in love, may have power, together with all the saints, to grasp how wide and long and high and deep is the love of Christ, and to know this love that surpasses knowledge—that I may be filled to the measure of all the fullness of God. Now to Him who is able to do immeasurably more than all we ask or imagine, according to His power that is at work within me, to Him be glory in the church and in Christ Jesus throughout all generations, for ever and ever! (Ephesians 3:14-21). In addition, I ask you dear heavenly Father, "Oh, that you would bless me and enlarge my territory! Let your hand be with me, and keep me from harm so that I will be free from pain" (1Chronicles 4:10). So, that I shall be free from poverty, sickness, disease, homelessness, hunger, unemployment, and any satanic attack that the enemy may try to form. O Sovereign LORD, you are God! Your words are trustworthy, and you have promised these good things to your servant (2 Samuel 7:28). Therefore, may the words of my mouth and the meditation of my heart be pleasing in your sight, O LORD, my Rock and my Redeemer (Psalm 19:14). In Jesus name, amen!

Understanding Fasting

Fasting is an excellent way of weakening the flesh to allow the "spirit man" to feed off the Word of God. The "spirit man" is the element that allows you to have a closer relationship with God; it's your connector and it must be fed the Word of God on a daily basis. Its very life support depends on the type of food it's fed. That's why it's imperative to select a bible that you can understand, one that has a cross-reference to provide further insight, a concordance to look up specific topics and a dictionary for those unfamiliar words. To further help in the growth and nourishment of the "spirit man", one must water it with daily prayer, worship and devotion.

I recently endured a 21-day consecration and it was powerful. During this fast, I reframed from white flour, white rice, pasta, red meat, sodas and anything that was pasteurized. I ate only fruits, nuts, vegetables, whole grain rice, wheat bread, chicken and fish. I drank only 100% fruit juices, soymilk, decaffeinated coffee and water. This fast is often referred to as the Daniel Fast (Daniel 10). In the middle of my fast, I felt empowered. By the end of the fast, I was on fire for Christ and preached like the Prophet Jeremiah.

You have to be lead by the Holy Spirit to begin fasting. You must also keep in mind any health conditions that may prevent you from restricting particular food. God wants us to use wisdom in all we do, so if you're diabetic, eat in moderations as not to put your health at risk. Always remember that it's not the length of the fast or the type of fast, but it's the sacrifice that has the greatest impact.

Also, food restriction is not the only form of fasting. You can fast by refusing to watch television, refuse to talk on the phone, or refuse to hang around certain people and opt instead to pray and read your bible. I have found all forms of fasting to be extremely beneficial to my walk with Christ.

God truly honors our sacrifice and the deeper connection that's established is indescribable.

May God bless you and your families as you endure to the end in search of Christ and His never changing love. May you seek Him as never before and His perfect will be made manifest in your life. We bind the enemy on every side of you, that you be all God originally attended for you. In Jesus name, amen.

My Testimony
(List the blessings and manifestations of God in your life)

_____
_____
_____
_____
_____
_____
_____
_____
_____
_____
_____
_____
_____
_____
_____
_____
_____
_____
_____
_____
_____
_____
_____
_____
_____
_____
_____
_____
_____
_____

Daily Affirmation of Faith:

1. I believe in the Power of God.

2. I believe in the Prosperity of the Lord.

3. I believe God is able.

4. I believe my every need is met with Heavens very best.

5. I believe the Word of God is living and active, able to do everything it sets out to accomplish.

6. I believe God's plans for my life will manifest.

7. I believe God's will for my life will be accomplished.

In the name of Jesus Christ, amen.